EUROPEAN MANAGEMENT GUIDES
General editor: Pete Burgess

Industrial relations

Incomes Data Services

Institute of Personnel Management

Phototypeset by The Comp-Room, Aylesbury, Buckinghamshire
and printed in Great Britain
by Short Run Press Ltd, Exeter, Devon

British Library cataloguing in publication data

Industrial relations. – (European management guides)
   I. Burgess, Pete   II. Incomes Data Services
   III. Series
   331.094

   ISBN 0-85292-453-4

The views expressed in this book are the author's own, and may not
necessarily reflect those of the Institute.

Contents

General Introduction

European Management Guides

The growing involvement of British business in the European Community has imposed novel demands on managers. For many small and medium-sized companies the challenge has been to find new markets and consolidate service networks. Larger organizations have been swept up in a series of mergers, acquisitions, joint ventures, strategic reviews and rationalization. In both cases, managers with personnel responsibilities have seen their tasks expanded and redefined. Increasingly, this includes involvement, both direct and at arm's length, in the recruitment and management of employees in other member states of the European Community. In many organizations the human resource manager has become the key figure in integrating the individuals and cultures which make up an internationalized company.

Experience has shown, often painfully, that the management of people lies at the heart of whether an international joint venture, merger or acquisition succeeds or fails. And familiarity with the local culture and regulation of employment underpins any understanding of the opportunities and limitations facing key executives in a foreign subsidiary. Acquisitions in particular, with their inheritance of established employment law and industrial relations practices, can pose a special challenge to new management teams.

The European Commission's plans for new Community legislation on many aspects of employment, as part of the 'social dimension' to the single European market, will bring national systems of employment law closer together. However, differences between cultures, institutions, law and practice will persist for the foreseeable future. Understanding and working with the grain of this diversity will be vital for any personnel or line manager entrusted with European responsibilities. Professional advice is indispensable in any European venture, but precious time and money can be saved by gathering information in advance before meeting lawyers, consultants or the local public authorities.

European Management Guides aim to meet this need for accessible and comprehensive information on employment in the countries of the European Community. The series, researched and written by Incomes Data Services Ltd, and published by the Institute of Personnel Management, consists of five handbooks covering:

- Recruitment.
- Terms and conditions of employment.
- Industrial relations.
- Pay and benefits.
- Training and development.

Each handbook will present information on a country-by-country basis, and will be structured to allow easy cross-country comparison. Extensive appendices detail local organizations which can provide further help and information. European Management Guides are not, however, intended as a substitute for expert advice, tailored to an individual situation and given as part of a professional relationship. Every effort has been made to ensure that the information contained in the handbooks is accurate and relevant. The publishers and authors offer them to readers on the understanding that neither organization seeks to take the place of either a lawyer or a consultant.

Incomes Data Services

Incomes Data Services has monitored employment developments in Europe since 1974. IDS's International Service publishers:

- *IDS European Report*, a monthly subscription journal on pay and employment law and practice in the European Community and Scandinavia. Each issue includes news on pay, collective bargaining and legal developments in Community countries, a Country Profile outlining recent developments, statistics and the economic background for individual countries, features, and regular statistics on pay, prices, labour costs and employment.
- *IDS International Documents*, two series of in-depth publications covering Commencement and Termination of Employment and Pay and Conditions on an individual country basis. Updated annually, each guide contains both context and detail for a single country in these central areas of human resource management.
- *1992: Personnel Management and the Single European Market*, published jointly with the Institute of Personnel Management.

For further details please contact: IDS Subscriptions, 193 St John Street, London EC1V 4LS (tel. 071-250 3434, fax 071-608 0949).

Acknowledgements

This handbook was researched and written by the International Department of Incomes Data Services Ltd, London. The series editor is Pete Burgess and other contributions were prepared by Angela Bowring, Andrea Broughton, Nana Mallet, Sally Marullo, Tony Morgan and Caroline Welch. The authors wish to thank Professor Rossetos Fakiolas for his contribution to the chapter on Greece, and Fernando Tempera (Lisbon) and Jorge Marques (APG, Lisbon) for their help and advice in preparing the Portuguese chapter. The authors are also grateful to the panel of expert advisers drawn from the national committees of the Institute of Personnel Management and to the IPM's Publications Department.

Introduction

Industrial relations in Europe

This is the third handbook in the five-volume IDS–IPM series of European Management Guides. Whereas the first and second volumes concentrated on the recruitment, terms and conditions of individual employees, this handbook sets out to deal with issues arising from how employers and employees relate to each other collectively within national systems of industrial relations. The main issues, covered on a country-by-country basis, are:

- Statutory and agreed systems of employee participation and representation.
- Trade union and employers' organizations.
- The bargaining structure.
- Industrial conflict.
- Collective dismissals and the transfer of undertakings.

The Handbook aims to provide an overview of the structures of industrial relations, and in particular to indicate any statutory or mandatory obligations on employers in the areas of employee participation, information disclosure and consultation, and where coverage through binding collective agreements may impose terms and conditions even on non-signatory organizations. How bargaining machinery operates in the collective determination of pay will be dealt with in the fourth volume of the series, covering pay and benefits. We do not attempt here to explore the 'cultural' dimensions of industrial relations nor to paint a detailed picture of workplace industrial relations in daily practice. Given the constraints of space, this would have inevitably been at the expense of presenting basic information on industrial relations structures which is often inaccessible in a convenient form in the English language. Moreover the danger of falling into, or borrowing, tendentious generalizations in this field is enormous. As the country chapters show, the degree of diversity within each national setting is very considerable, evidenced in widely varying degrees of trade unionism or practice on employee participation by industry, region and, primarily, by company size. Readers who wish to delve into comparisons of management styles and practices will find an excellent overview of the issues in *Management and Labour in Europe* by Christel Lane, which also offers a substantial bibliography (see Further Reading).

Diversity and difference

The pattern of industrial relations in the ten countries of the European Community dealt with in this handbook is a very diverse one: there is no 'Continental model' of industrial relations. And, as with the UK system, each national system in Europe is the product of national histories and cultures, many of which have embraced traumatic convulsions directly bearing on industrial relations. Structures of employee participation, for example, have rarely been drawn up as rational models but have typically been the product of and response to periods of political and industrial strife: works councils in Germany were born out of the 1918 revolution, the first initiatives in France emerged during the 1930s Popular Front, and workplace industrial relations in Italy were crucially shaped by the 'hot autumn' of 1969 and its accompanying social turbulence. It is important for UK personnel specialists operating within these systems to be aware that the protagonists are conscious of their broader setting, and in the case of more recent developments in Spain, Greece and Portugal may well have been directly involved.

These national differences are particularly marked, for example, in levels of *trade union density* – 75–80 per cent in Belgium and Denmark, about 35–40 per cent in Germany and Italy, and only 10–15 per cent (and perhaps less) in Spain and France. Nonetheless, mechanisms for extending collective agreements by law to organizations and employees who were not party to them means that the coverage of the workforce by such terms can be much greater than these figures suggest. (In the case of France and Spain, for example, agreements are estimated to apply to approximately 80 per cent of the workforce.)

The incidence of industrial disputes also varies very considerably, although comparisons are plagued by difficulties of definition. In 1987, for example, there was a range extending from 2 days lost per 1,000 employees in Germany to 325 days in the Irish Republic.

Common to all EC members states, however, has been a steady fall-off in industrial action during the 1980s.

Employee participation

However, one area in which continental Europe as a whole offers a marked contrast to the UK is that of employee participation. Most EC members states have some form of statutory provision or agreed system with widespread coverage. The precise mechanisms for employee participation range from statutory systems with extensive and detailed powers for worker representatives, as in the Netherlands and Germany, to systems built on national-level collective agreements with more broadly defined obligations, as in Denmark and Italy. Nevertheless, whereas the German works council system stands out in terms of the formal rights accorded to employee representatives, which include consultation on all hiring and firing, the fact that works councils are not mandatory means that by no means all employers operate within this framework.

Even where the setting up of structures of employee representation is mandatory, with the responsibility falling on the employer, as in France, employee apathy and employer hostility or resort to alternative industrial relations arrangements can often mean that the law is ignored or its operation weakened. Nevertheless, although personnel practitioners in continental Europe are more accustomed than their UK counterparts to managing within a legally regulated industrial environment, in which statutory or virtually universally binding participation plays a large part, this difference from the UK should not be overstated in terms of its practical impact. A study of staff representation in France, carried out by the French Ministry of Labour, found that regular consultation took place in only 10–15 per cent of works committees and that nearly 20 per cent of companies with between fifty and ninety-nine employees had no works committee at all, despite the fact that these are obligatory in companies with fifty or more employees. In contrast, a 1990 survey of consultation and communication in British companies conducted by the UK Advisory, Conciliation and Arbitration Service (ACAS) found that some 40 per cent of surveyed establishments had joint consultative committees, supplemented by other mechanisms such as joint working parties. Levels of informal participation and influence on managerial decision-making in the UK are also widely held to be higher than under more formalized systems, such as the German one, and may afford employees greater power at the workplace and on job control issues than a panoply of formal but under-used statutory rights.

Nonetheless, enforceable rights to information about corporate developments and, in Germany and the Netherlands, the right of employee representatives to resort to the courts to prevent or delay managerial decisions in areas regarded as within management's prerogative in the UK can prove at best a novelty and at worst a shock to a manager with a British or American background. Both these systems are, however, characterized by a high level of consensus between unions and management on many industrial fundamentals, and are part of wider structures in which employee representatives at plant level do not play a direct part in pay negotiation, removing a good deal of the raw material for conflict from the immediate workplace.

European Community law and proposals

European Community law in the collective sphere is currently confined to directives on collective redundancies (75/129/EEC) and on the safeguarding of employees' rights in the event of transfers of undertakings (77/187/EEC). Both provide for consultation with employee representatives, and in many member states are already embraced by and improved on in national legislation. The EC's framework directive on improving health and safety at the workplace (89/391/EEC) also provides for employee representation 'in accordance with national laws and practices': the rights of health and safety representatives are indicated in the individual country chapters. In addition to the information and consultation rights in directives 75/129 and 77/187, this framework directive adds an element of employee participation in the formulation and implementation of health and safety policies. These are more precisely defined in specific directives issued under the framework legislation.

The 1975 directive on collective redundancies, implemented in the UK through Part IV of the Employment Protection Act 1975, requires employers contemplating collective redundancies to consult employee representatives; consultations must include ways and means of avoiding redundancies, reducing the number of workers affected and mitigating the consequences. Relevant information must be made available to employee representatives, with the reasons in writing for the redundancies, the numbers of workers to be made redundant, the number of workers normally employed, and the period over which redundancies are to be effected. (Each of the country chapters details the specific national procedures to be followed in conjunction with local systems of employee representation.) Further EC proposals to ensure the effective implementation of the directive in cross-border redundancy situations are expected to be published before the end of 1991.

The 1977 directive on transfers of undertakings, implemented in the UK through the Transfer of Undertakings Regulations 1981, seeks to safeguard employees' rights in the event of transfers of undertakings by providing that the rights and obligations of an employer transferring the business pass to the new employer, and by ruling that a transfer does not in itself provide grounds for dismissal. The directive makes two main provisions in the field of collective rights. First, it requires that the status and function of employee representatives or employee representation should not be affected by the transfer, provided the business preserves its autonomy. Second, it grants information and consultation rights to affected employees. Article 6 of the directive requires both the transferor and the transferee to inform representatives of their respective employees affected by a transfer of:

- The reasons for the transfer.
- The legal, economic and social implications of the transfer for the employees.
- Measures envisaged in relation to the employees.

Measures advanced under the single European market programme would, if adopted, add to the scope of EC legislation making provision for employee information and consultation rights. The two main proposals currently concern (1) consultation machinery under proposals for a Regulation on a European Company Statute, originally conceived in 1970 but given extra impetus by the single market, and (2) proposals for a European works council in large multinational organizations made under the 1989 Social Charter. Two other proposals for information and consultation rights pre-date the single market and Social Charter. They are the draft 'Fifth Directive', which would provide for employee representation on major decisions in large companies, either through worker representatives on company boards, works councils or other equivalent arrangements, and the 'Vredeling Directive', intended to provide for information and consultation rights in companies with 1,000 or more workers. Whereas the Fifth Directive is still under discussion (see below), the controversial Vredeling proposals have now been effectively but not wholly superseded by the proposals for a European works council. The main elements of each proposal are outlined below:

European company statute. The proposal for a European company statute aims to offer firms the possibility of incorporation at European level through the creation of a European company, or SE (*societas Europaea*). This would, the Commission hopes, foster the creation of groups consisting of companies from various European countries and enable cross-border operations to be handled more easily, encouraging the development of a more integrated European economy. One inducement for companies to register themselves as an SE would be the ability to set off losses in one country against profits elsewhere. The proposed regulation, the most recent draft of which was released in July 1991, establishing the SE and binding on any company adopting SE status is accompanied by a draft directive on employee involvement in such companies. Any SE would be required to establish one of three proposed systems set out in the draft to ensure that employees could participate in the 'supervision and strategic development' of the SE. The models offered by the draft are:

- The appointment and removal of employee representatives to the supervisory or administrative board of the company, with employee representatives making up at least one-third and not more than half of each body.
- The establishment of a 'separate body', equivalent to a works council, which would have to be informed of the progress and prospects of the SE's business every three months. Information which might have 'significant implications' for the SE's situation would have to be supplied without delay.

- 'Other models' could be established by agreement, with employee representatives afforded the same information rights as with a works council structure. Where no agreement is possible, a standard model to be provided by national law in the country where the SE has its registered office would apply, but would guarantee the same rights of information and consultation.

Certain decisions would not be allowed to be taken without prior consultation with employee representatives. These include:

- Setting up, acquisition, disposal or closing down of the undertaking or parts of the business where the purchase price or proceeds from disposal exceed a percentage of subscribed capital in the business, to be determined by the SE's statutes but which may not be more than 25 per cent or less than 5 per cent.
- Raising or granting loans on the same scale.
- The conclusion of supply or performance contracts, involving sums which exceed the threshold stated above.

The European company statute regulation has been submitted under article 100A of the Treaty of Rome, and is therefore subject to qualified majority voting (see the introduction to the second Volume in the European Management Guides series). The proposed directive is based on Article 24, which deals with freedom of establishment and also requires a qualified majority. The proposed implementation date is 31 December 1993.

Fifth Directive. The draft Fifth Directive is concerned with establishing EC regulation on structures of company law for large undertakings at national level (see below), together with a set of rights for employee involvement. Under the 1988 draft of the directive, companies with more than 1,000 employees would be required to provide information to employee representatives every three months on the progress and prospects of the company, with consultation rights before major decisions. (These information and consultation rights closely parallel those envisaged in the European company statute proposal). Although the draft is still under discussion, it would require unanimity, and the proposal is not regarded as having a strong chance of being adopted in its current form.

European Works Council. The proposal for employee information and consultation in Community-scale undertakings and groups of undertakings was issued in December 1990, and would require the unanimous agreement of member states in the Council of Ministers. It aims to provide for information rights in companies with at least 1,000 employees within the European Community and at least two establishments in different member states, each employing at least 100 persons. Employees would be entitled to form a European Works Council (EWC) whose composition and powers would be settled by agreement between the management of the undertaking and a negotiating body formed by the group's or undertaking's employees. The EWC would have the right to meet the undertaking's central management at least once a year to be informed of the progress and prospects of the business, including information on the firm's financial situation, employment trends and investments. The EWC would also have to be informed of any management proposals likely to have serious consequences for the work force, and would have a right to give its opinion on the decision.

European works councils

A number of companies have been operating information and consultation bodies at European level for some years, and these have gained considerable impetus from EC proposals in this area. A number of recently agreed European forums or works councils, such as those agreed at Bayer or Elf-Aquitaine, expressly refer to EC proposals. According to a study of existing arrangements carried out under the auspices of the European Foundation for the Improvement of Living and Working Conditions (see Further Reading), such bodies have been spreading quite slowly in recent years, are confined to a small number of multinational enterprises, and tend to be still operating on a trial basis. Most provide opportunities only for information disclosure, with rare provision for consultation. None represents a forum for negotiation.

The mechanisms by which these bodies have been established and operate vary from formal agreements (Bull, Thomson) or informal arrangements (Allianz, Nestlé, St Gobain) to *ad hoc* exchange visits (Ford, IBC) and union-only panels (Airbus, Gillette). Most provide for an annual meeting, with the costs borne by the group. According to the European Foundation study, managements (who were found to be generally positive towards the operation of the bodies) cited the benefits as: enabling them to explain corporate strategy, facilitating company restructuring and creating a corporate 'sense of belonging'.

Issues related to European-level collective bargaining will be discussed in Volume 4 of this series dealing with mechanisms of pay determination.

1

Belgium

Belgian industrial relations are characterized by a remarkable degree of consensus, embodied in the various joint bodies established at all levels to regulate the labour environment, in addition to a highly developed collective bargaining system. This consensus has its origins in the 1944 social solidarity pact agreed between employers and trade union groupings under the Occupation, which laid down the principles and methods of joint co-operation, and became the predominant philosophy in the post-war years.

A clear distinction is drawn between consultation and bargaining activity – arrangements for both being well regulated, although in practice their functions sometimes overlap; some bodies have responsibility in both areas. For example, the National Labour Council, which consists of employer and union representatives and is chaired by a Crown appointee, has both a consultative and an advisory role, as well as responsibility for bargaining (see below). This duality is mirrored, although to a lesser extent, in the activities of joint industry committees and consultation bodies at company level, where employees may hold office on more than one type of committee.

The government plays a complementary role in industrial relations, preferring initially to leave employers and trade unions to make their own arrangements within a well defined framework. A substantial body of labour law exists, and proposals for new legislation must be submitted to the National Labour Council for consultation. It is unlikely that the government would proceed with a Bill which met with a generally unfavourable reaction. Labour laws are supplemented and complemented by a comprehensive web of legally binding collective agreements, concluded at the various levels. Employers seem able to operate within this framework and to adapt the system to their needs. The joint bodies at company level are generally regarded as useful and effective channels of communication.

One major criticism of the consensus approach is that the

1

outcome of talks is usually some form of compromise, with no clear policy objective. However, it is generally agreed that the industrial relations system works well, if a trifle bureaucratically. One principle reason for its effectiveness concerns the role of organized labour. Trade unions have been institutionalized in the system, both in bipartite bodies and as recognized bargaining agents. Since trade union membership is high, at approximately 70 per cent of the labour force, unions are representative and can operate in a highly organized and disciplined way which can often head off open conflict. Owing to their important role in the scheme of things, unions place great emphasis on training their representatives to carry out their duties properly.

Consultation at national level

National Labour Council

The National Labour Council (*Conseil National du Travail*), often called Belgium's 'social parliament', plays a pivotal role in industrial relations. Set up in 1952 as a bipartite body, it comprises twenty-four members, half from the three employers' organizations and half from among the three trade union confederations deemed to be representative nationally. To qualify for a seat on the council, unions must demonstrate a membership of at least 50,000. (This threshold serves to discourage fragmentation but has been challenged at the ILO on the grounds that more objective criteria are needed to define a representative trade union.) An independent chair, usually an industrial relations specialist, is nominated by the Crown.

The following organizations currently sit on the council: for the employers' side, the Federation of Belgian Enterprises, one organization representing small and medium-sized enterprises, and a representative from the agricultural organizations; and on the employees' side, the three trade unions confederations, the CSC, FGTB and CGSLB, which are considered representative nationally.

The National Labour Council's original role was consultative, and this continues through advice (in the form of a recommendation or *avis*) to Ministers or Parliament on social matters where regulation is proposed or needs clarification; this may either be requested by the politicians or carried out on its own initiative. It can also examine an issue at the request of either side of industry.

The council may make recommendations on jurisdictional disputes between the individual joint sectoral committees (*commissions paritaires*) responsible for bargaining at industry level – for example, where their coverage overlaps. In addition, the council may also recommend the creation of joint committees where new activities have become established – for example, for non-profit-making organizations.

Some individual Acts of Parliament specifically give the council the right to advise on matters within the scope of the law. For example, the 1978 contracts of employment legislation gives the council the right to advise on days off for family events (*petits chômages*).

The Act of December 1968 on collective bargaining and joint committees empowered the council to conclude binding nationwide collective agreements (*conventions collectives de travail*) which are signed by all nationally representative trade unions. These normally cover the whole private sector but sometimes apply only to individual branches of activity (see below). In the first instance, such agreements are binding only on organizations affiliated to the signatory bodies, that is, on those employers' organizations and trade union confederations represented on the council. However, such agreements can be extended by royal decree at the request of the signatory parties to become generally legally binding.

The council may also conclude collective agreements on behalf of joint committees which do not function fully (such as for temporary workers) or for those few sectors of the economy where no bargaining machinery has been established.

The council operates on a consensual basis, with members acting under mandate from their organizations but referring back where appropriate. The council aims at joint regulation of employment matters without government intervention. However, if progress on an issue is slow, the government may announce or introduce draft legislation to speed discussion along. It adopted the latter strategy when talks about a framework agreement for shift and night work looked as if they might flounder. Some three-quarters of the council's recommendations are unanimous; it has issued over 1,000 to date. The council is assisted by a secretariat. Most matters are dealt with in *ad hoc* fashion by a specific working party on which two council members sit; experts from both employers' and union organizations participate in the negotiations. A full council session is held only when there is a clear question to be decided, such as the submission on a proposed parliamentary Bill. In full session the council is assisted by experts from the appropriate working parties and outside specialists when drafting texts.

Central Economic Council

The National Labour Council has no formal links with its sister organization in the economic field, although there is frequent co-operation based on a 1983 protocol. The Central Economic Council (*Conseil Central de l'Economie*) comprises fifty members, twenty-two from each side of industry, with six experts and an independent chair. The Economic Council operates in a less consensual way than the National Labour Council. Its role has recently been revitalized, since under the 1989 law on industrial competitiveness it is charged with producing a regular twice-yearly report on Belgium's comparative position *vis-á-vis* its seven principle competitors on which the social partners must give their view. If the country's position is unfavourable, according to a set of defined indicators, the government could resort to special powers to intervene in the economy, including modifying the country's automatic pay indexation system.

Consultation at workplace level

There are three types of body at company level, whose roles are split between consultation on the one hand and bargaining on the other. Two of these – the works council and the health and safety committee – are statutory joint bodies with a primarily consultative function. The third, the trade union delegation, unlike the others established by collective agreement, comprises solely trade union representatives who fulfil a bargaining role. Often employees hold office on more than one body.

These bodies exist at establishment level (*unité technique d'exploitation*), as defined by law. Thus a company might have, for example, several works councils functioning in different establishments within a company. And although there would normally be liaison between them, there is no provision in law for a co-ordinating structure. There are instances where companies have organized themselves so as to avoid the setting up of systems of representations.

Works councils

The establishment and functioning of works councils (*conseils d'entreprise*) is governed by an Act of 20 September 1948 (*loi portant sur l'organisation de l'économie*), by agreements made with individual joint sector committees, and by each council's own standing orders. A number of agreements concluded within the National Labour Council, notably collective agreement No. 9, also elaborate upon certain aspects of works councils, such as the financial information which must be disclosed.

Composition. Works councils must be set up on the initiative of the employer in all establishments employing on average at least 100 workers. All workers employed under a contract of employment or apprenticeship, even temporaries, with at least three months' service are taken into account when calculating the size of the establishment's work force. Employees working less than full time count as the equivalent of half an employee.

Works councils are joint bodies chaired by the employer. Apart from the head of the company, the employer side comprises employer nominees, who may not outnumber the employee side. Employee-side members are elected by secret ballot in the private sector every four years over a period declared by decree for the whole country; there is separate representation for blue and white-collar staff and for young workers, provided there are at least twenty-five, and managers (if fifteen at least are employed by the firm – see below).

Information rights. The works council must be given information on a wide range of economic, financial and social matters. At the first meeting of a new council it must be supplied with basic data on the company's legal status, its financial structure, its investment plans, the volume and value of production and productivity rates, and wage and labour costs. The standing orders must also be approved.

Each year the works council must consider a written report on the company's financial position, the profit and loss account, and the auditor's report. The works council takes part in the selection of an auditor, who may attend meetings and must assist if called upon to do so by a majority of the members. Every three months information must be provided on orders, sales, costs and prices, and employment. The works council must also be advised of any company plans which could have an impact on the work force, for example the introduction of new technology or a proposed takeover.

These information rights are broadly respected. Trade unions have their own experts to assist with the interpretation of data, and auditors have a much more independent role than previously. Unions put considerable effort into training their representatives to carry out these functions.

Council members are bound by confidentiality and may be specifically requested to withhold particularly sensitive information from the rest of the work force. It is also possible for employers to obtain the authorization of the labour authorities to withhold information of a highly confidential or prejudicial nature.

Consultation rights. The works council has a general right to be consulted and give advice on any measure affecting working conditions and work organization and on personnel practices in general. Reports on the employment situation must be submitted on a quarterly and annual basis, with consultation taking place on proposed measures such as criteria for recruitment and dismissal, arrangements for the induction of new recruits, and consultation over collective training and retraining.

Decision-making rights. The works council may also take decisions in certain areas. There are differences of opinion over whether these have to be unanimous to be valid; a works council's own standing orders will often clarify the position, and there is also case law. The areas include:

- Internal works rules.
- Methods of paying salaries.
- Criteria for hiring temporary staff.

- Criteria for selecting employees for redundancy.
- Setting the dates of annual holidays and alternative days off when a public holiday falls on a Sunday.
- Managing the enterprise's social funds.

The works council may assume the functions of the health and safety committee under certain circumstances.

Because the role of works councils is quite wide and encompasses matters such as the organization of production, initiatives such as quality circles and total quality management, have not become a normal part of the industrial relations scene, although they do exist and encounter trade union apprehension.

Meetings. The works council meetings take place on company premises, normally within normal working hours. Meetings must take place at least monthly, or at the request either of the chair (the head of the company or deputy) or at least half the works council's members.

Election of works councils. The electoral processes for both works councils and health and safety committees are similar though distinct and they are conducted at the same time. The procedure is complex and we simply set out the main points below (a number of comprehensive guides are available).

In 1991 over a million employees were eligible to vote for members of the employee side of the works council, which generally represent both unionized and non-unionized employees. The criteria for calculating the size of an establishment's work force (see above) are also used to define entitlement to vote. Senior management can neither nominate candidates nor participate in the elections of employee representatives. There are separate electoral colleges for blue-collar workers and white-collar employees. If there are at least twenty-five employees under the age of 25, then separate seats are reserved for them. In works council elections, managers qualify for separate representation through their own electoral college only if they number at least fifteen members. They have no separate representation on health and safety committees.

The electoral process must be carried out in the appropriate language, according to the region where the firm is situated – broadly, Flemish in Flanders, French in Wallonia, either language in Brussels, depending on local criteria, and German in some of the eastern provinces.

Trade unions affiliated to confederations which are deemed representative on a national basis, in practice the CSC, FGTB and CGSLB, have a monopoly on presenting lists, and the election outcome is seen as a test of the popularity of the various organizations. To qualify as candidates, employees must be employed by the firm, aged between 18 and retirement age (16–25 for youth candidates), have six months' service and belong to the occupational group for which they are standing. There would be nothing to prevent a non-unionist appearing on a union list, but it rarely happens. The number of employee seats ranges from six (in firms with 101 employees) to eight in firms with up to 1,000 employees, and to twenty-two for firms with 8,000 employees or more. There are either one or two management seats where there are between fifteen and ninety-nine managers. The allocation of seats as between blue and white-collar employees varies according to their relative numbers, as do those reserved for young workers. Each union may present a list comprising candidates (and their reserves) equal to the total number of seats to be voted upon. There are precise rules governing the replacement of a member by a reserve.

The result must be published within two days of the election, together with details of the management side of the council.

Status of works council members. The law provides that employee representatives should be given sufficient time off within normal working hours to fulfil their duties. This is often further defined by industry agreement. Time off is paid at normal rates. Members also have a right to circulate freely within the enterprise. Works council and health and safety committee members are protected against dismissal, except for genuine redundancy or serious misconduct. In either case, the proposed termination must meet a set of stringent criteria and be accepted by a joint committee or labour tribunal.

Health and safety committees

The establishment and functioning of health and safety committees (*comités de securité, d'hygiène et d'embellissement des lieux de travail* – often abbreviated to *comités* SHE) are regulated by the law of 10 June 1952 (*concernant la santé et la securité des travailleurs*), articles 54 and 837–9 of the 1947 General Regulations for the Protection of Work (*Règlement général pour la protection du travail*, RGPT) and national collective agreement No. 6 on facilities for works councils and health and safety committee members.

All establishments employing an average of fifty workers, both in the private and in the public sectors, must set up a health and safety committee comprising an equal number of employer and employee representatives.

Composition. As mentioned above, the employee side is elected on the same basis as works council members, except that there is no separate managerial representation; however, the separate representation of white-collar, blue-collar and youth employee groups remains the same. The size of the employee side ranges from four members in establishments with fewer than 100 workers to twenty-two in those with a work force of 8,000 or more.

The employer side must include the head of the company, who chairs the committee. The works doctor has an independent consultative non-voting role, whilst the head of the firm's health and safety service does have a vote although acting in an independent capacity.

Rights. The committees' functions are defined by the RGPT and involve being informed and consulted on all matters relating to health and safety in the workplace. Great emphasis is placed on the prevention of risks and on the active promotion of health and safety. The committee is deemed competent to take decisions, make recommendations and obtain information in all these areas. The head of the firm's health and safety services may not be appointed or dismissed without the approval of the committee. It can also demand the dismissal of the works doctor if it is dissatisfied with the way his or her duties are being discharged.

Meetings. Meetings must be held at least monthly, or at the request of the chair or of a third of the committee's members. Members may be assisted by outside experts. The head of the firm must submit for the committee's approval a draft annual plan to promote health and safety. If a complaint is lodged by any member of the work force against the employer, they have the right to express their point of view. Under certain circumstances, the labour inspectorate can call a meeting and chair it.

Trade union delegations

These, the other arm of employee work place representation, are dealt with in the section on collective bargaining below, as their role lies primarily in that area.

Trade unions

Trade union law

Freedom of association is guaranteed by law. This gives the individual a right to join or not to join a trade union of their choice, and means that the closed shop does not exist.

Trade unions have no status in law, that is, they are *de facto* organizations; however, they are recognized for certain purposes and the law does make stipulations about their representativeness (see below). Belgian trade unions have so far successfully resisted all attempts at conferring legal status on them, since they believe it would restrict their freedom of action. They cannot be sued for damages, nor as an organization can a union be served with an injunction (see below).

In order to be considered nationally representative, and entitled to sit on the National Labour Council, trade union confederations must demonstrate that they have inter-industry membership of at least 50,000. They are not required to register and may set their own rules. A union affiliated to any one of the three nationally representative confederations is entitled to sign collective agreements.

Trade union structure

The trade union situation is marked by a high degree of pluralism. Most organized workers belong to a union affiliated to one of the three nationally representative trade union confederations. These represent three distinct political strands, although neither of the two major centres has a formal link with a political party. Confederations co-ordinate the strategy and work of their constituent union federations.

All are organized along both industry and geographical lines, with a distinct organization according to the three main regions of the country.

The General Federation of Belgian Workers (*Fédération Générale du Travail de Belgique, FGTB*) is socialist-oriented and started as a trade union grouping within the organization which eventually become the Socialist Party. Although now formally separate, the FGTB cooperates closely with the Socialist Party. It adopted its present form in 1945. It now has over a million members spread evenly over the two main regions of the country.

The Confederation of Christian Trade Unions of Belgium (*Confédération des Syndicats Chrétiens de Belgique, CSC*), which represents the Christian socialist strand in the trade union movement, was formed as a confederation in 1912. It had its origins in an anti-socialist trade union alliance and places particular emphasis on family values and reconciliation between work and family responsibilities. The confederation has well over a million members and its influence is strongest in Flanders.

The smallest national confederation, the General Confederation of Liberal Trade Unions of Belgium (*Centrale Générale des Syndicats Libéraux de Belgique, CGSLB*), with a Liberal philosophy, was established in 1930 and recognized as a representative union in 1946: it has some 200,000 members.

The National Confederation of Managers (*Confédération Nationale des Cadres, CNC*) has been recognized as nationally representative of managers for the purpose of forming a separate college for works council elections. However, it is not recognized as representative in other respects and has not been granted a seat on the National Labour Council, despite repeated applications. Managers are also represented by the other main union confederations.

The FGTB and CSC are both organized along industry lines for manual workers in the private sector, with separate federations crossing industry boundaries for white-collar staff. The CGSLB has no industry federations.

There are a small number of autonomous national trade unions whose influence is limited.

Union membership is high, with a density estimated at 60–70 per cent of the work force, with 60 per cent of private-sector employees and 90 per cent of public-sector employees in trade unions. Around 50 per cent of white-collar and 70–80 per cent of blue-collar workers are organized. Check-off is rare and membership dues are either collected in the work place or deducted by standing order. Unions hold strike funds. Because trade unions fulfil an important role in systems of both consultation and bargaining, trade union training is an important issue and one often regulated by industry collective agreement.

Employers' organizations

There is no obligation on employers to join a federation to promote their interests. Like trade unions, employers' federations have not tended to opt for constitution as a legal entity, although some affiliates of the largest federation have done so.

The Federation of Belgian Enterprises (*Fédération des Entreprises de Belgique, FEB*) is the main employers' confederation, representing members in both manufacturing and services. Constituted in its present form in 1973, it comprises three inter-industry organizations, according to the country's three regions, and is estimated to account for organizations employing approximately a million workers.

Small commercial, craft and industrial firms are represented in a separate organization.

Collective bargaining

The 1968 Act on collective agreements and joint sectoral committees (*loi sur les conventions collectives de travail et les commissions paritaires*) recognizes and defines collective agreements, which are legally enforceable, and specifies the various levels at which such agreements can be concluded.

Definition of a collective agreement

According to the Act a collective agreement is an agreement between one or more workers' organizations and one or more organizations representing employers, or alternatively one or more employers, which governs individual and collective work relations and lays down respective rights and obligations. Such an agreement may either be concluded within a joint body (that is, the National Labour Council, the joint sectoral committees, or their sub-committees – set up by main committees) or outside it, at company level.

An agreement must be in writing and in both Flemish and French, except when it covers a geographical area where only one language is spoken. Representatives signing agreements are presumed competent to do so on behalf of their respective organizations; when concluding company agreements, union representatives must be mandated to do so by their unions, although often a district official will sign. Agreements may be concluded for either a definite or an indefinite period. Notice to terminate must also be given in writing. The agreement must specify:

- The signatory parties.
- In appropriate cases the number of the joint sectoral committee.
- Its coverage (sector, area, occupational group, company).
- Its duration.
- The implementation date (if not the date of signature).

An agreement concluded in a joint body must be registered with the Ministry of Labour, where a copy can be obtained on payment of a sum fixed by law. Company agreements do not have to be registered, although many often are, so as to establish that specific expenditure (for example, on training) required by law or agreement has been undertaken. Notification of collective agreements is published in Belgium's official journal, *Moniteur Belge*.

At the request of the appropriate joint body, or a party represented on it, a collective agreement can be extended by royal decree to become generally binding in its entirety on all employers within the defined area. An employer may wish to take on the terms of an agreement, for example where it covers their sector but has not been generally extended. Such a request would normally be conceded, provided the signatory parties do not object: reasons must be given for a refusal. Details of these association arrangements are also published in the official journal.

Hierarchy of collective provisions

The 1968 legislation sets out the hierarchy of legal sources and
obligations governing working relations as follows:

- Law.
- Collective agreement which has been extended. In descending
  order of priority these are those concluded: (a) within the
  National Labour Council, (b) within a joint sectoral committee,
  and (c) within a joint sectoral sub-committee.
- A collective agreement concluded at any of these three levels
  which has not been extended but is still legally binding on their
  signatories and their affiliates.
- Other collective agreements, that is, those concluded at company
  or plant level.
- The individual contract of employment.

An agreement, or individual contract, may not contain any
provision which contravenes a term agreed at a higher level.

Collective agreements are binding on members of signatory
organizations and on those organizations which adhere to them,
either from the date of signature or from the date of adherence to
the agreement, or from another date specified by the agreement
itself. Parties can go to court to enforce the normative clauses of
agreements, that is, those elements determining pay, hours and
other conditions.

Levels of bargaining

An agreement concluded with a joint body must be reached
between all organizations represented on it. Although a single
union could sign a company agreement, in practice unions act
jointly where more than one is represented in an enterprise. The
official journal, *Moniteur Belge*, not only publicizes brief details of
such agreements but also notifies when parties wish to terminate them.

National agreements (accords interprofessionels). Periodically –
in practice usually every other year – the main employers'
organizations and the three trade union confederations negotiate
a national agreement on various issues which sets guidelines for

bargainers at sectoral and company levels. The latest agreement, covering 1991 and 1992, focuses on the protection of company competitiveness and the promotion of jobs and training. These agreements are not collective agreements in the legal sense and are therefore morally rather than legally binding. However, specific terms may become subject to regulation, either directly through legislation – as was the case with the additional fifteenth week of maternity leave granted as from 1991 – or through the conclusion of a collective agreement within the National Labour Council.

National collective agreements. As mentioned above, the National Labour Council concludes collective agreements (each given a number) which are initially binding on signatory parties, though the vast majority are subsequently rendered mandatory on the whole private sector by royal decree. Since 1968 around fifty such agreements have been signed – many of them since subject to considerable amendment. They include such issues as collective dismissal (see below), a guaranteed minimum monthly wage, equal pay, part-time work, temporary and casual work, the status of work place trade union delegations, and information and consultation on the introduction of new technology.

Agreements can be identified by breaking down the various codes attached to their official designations. For example, CCT No. 42 (*convention collective de travail*) *sur l'introduction de nouveaux régimes de travail dans les entreprises* 02 06 1987, AR 18 06 1987, MB 26 06 1987 refers to collective agreement No. 42 on the introduction of new working time schedules in companies, concluded on 2 June 1987, extended by royal decree on 18 June and published in the official journal, the *Moniteur Belge*, on 26 June.

Industry bargaining. Bipartite joint industry committees (*commissions paritaires*), responsible for collective bargaining at sector level, were set up after the First World War, initially in the iron and steel, mining and engineering industries.

Joint committees

The 1968 legislation on collective agreements and joint committees provides for the formation of a joint committee for every sector of activity in the private sector, outlining the procedure for instituting joint committees and sub-committees and the scope of their activities according to branch, regional and occupational group (that is, blue-collar, white-collar or both). Around 100 committees and 70 sub-committees exist, covering around 90 per cent of the private sector. New employers can ascertain from the Ministry of Labour, or the labour inspectorate, which joint committee covers their business, as they may be bound by terms negotiated in it. Identifying the correct joint committee is not a matter of employer choice and is strictly regulated.

The size of each joint committee is defined by law and comprises a chair, a vice-chair, an equal number of representatives defined by law from employer and employee organizations, and two or more secretaries. The committee's term of office lasts four years. Meetings must be attended by at least half the members and decisions must be taken unanimously.

The main role of joint committees may be summarized as follows:

- Conclusion of collective agreements between all the organizations represented on the committee in order to regulate pay and working conditions.
- Prevention and settlement of disputes between employers and employees.
- Advising the government, the National Labour Council, the Central Economic council and local trade councils on issues falling within their scope.
- Management of sectoral social security funds (*fonds de securité sociale*) where these exist.

Industry agreements cover an enormous range of issues besides pay and working hours: the induction of new recruits, trade union training, the work place trade union delegation, the standing orders of works councils (see below), apprenticeships, career breaks, early retirement, temporary employment, levels of employment.

Company-level bargaining and trade union delegations. Trade union delegations (*délégations syndicales*) are established under the provisions of a national collective agreement (No. 5) and comprise only trade union representatives. They have a bargaining role.

Originally recognized by a national agreement in 1947, later replaced by national collective agreement No. 5, agreed within the National Labour Council in 1971, the status and rights of trade union delegations are also regulated by industry, and on occasion company, agreement. Since the delegation is regulated by a binding agreement, recognition of a trade union does not normally constitute an issue for the individual employer.

A delegation may be established in any firm if one or more unions affiliated to nationally representative centres request it. A joint sectoral agreement often lays down the rules governing the establishment of a delegation, including thresholds of the number of workers necessary to qualify, required union density, number of delegates, manner of appointment, and delegates' time off. Delegates may be appointed by their union members or elected; in the latter case, elections may be timed to coincide with elections for works councils and health and safety committees. The work place trade union delegation is the recognized channel through which workers make their demands and negotiate with the employer. Delegations are recognized as competent to sign agreements provided they have a mandate from the trade unions of which they are members, although often a district union official will be the signatory.

The principle object of a trade union committee is the defence of workers' interests through:

- Regular bargaining, leading to the conclusion of collective agreements within the company.
- Monitoring the implementation of labour legislation generally in the company, including whether trade union rights are being respected.
- Undertaking the functions of a works council or health and safety committee if none exists.

Trade union delegations are also entitled to become involved in the prevention and resolution of grievances, whether of an individual or of a collective nature; this implies having access to the employer. They can also call in full-time trade union officials, as can the employer.

As a consequence, trade union delegations have an extensive right to information, particularly concerning changes in working

conditions. Delegates are able to communicate with the work
force through meetings, which may be working time, or notice
boards and in premises put at their disposal by the employer.
Delegates enjoy some protection against dismissal for the duration
of their mandate (four years renewable). However, the criteria are
not as stringent as in the case of works and health and safety
committee members.

Industrial conflict

Industrial conflict is regulated and formalized by peace obligations
in collective agreements. Since these concern the procedural
aspects of the agreement, they are not legally enforceable *per
se*, but constitute an implied obligation on the parties. A social
harmony clause specifies that no collective or individual claims
may be introduced in respect of issues covered by the agreement
during its life span. Most agreements specify a period of notice
for termination. The harmony obligation is usually respected, and
the number of strikes is small. An obligation to implement the
contract in accordance with its terms is also an implied term, which
means signatories have to persuade their affiliates to abide by all
its provisions.

Conciliation

Each joint sectoral committee has a conciliation committee (*bureau
de conciliation*) usually presided over by the sectoral committee
chair. This committee is responsible for the interpretation of an
agreement and can intervene at the request of the employer or
trade unions. Conciliation meetings normally take place at the
Ministry of Labour, but are sometimes convened elsewhere. It is
up to the committee to decide on the procedure for conciliation
in terms of whether a joint or separate meeting of the parties
should take place. The latter course of action is adopted when
initial viewpoints are far apart. The conciliation procedure is used
to positive effect.

The right to strike

There is no specific statutory right to strike. However, international law and conventions providing for the right to strike, including the European Social Charter, offer to provide some legal basis where ratified.) In addition the right to strike has been recognized by case law. A 1981 Supreme Court ruling on 1948 legislation providing for the maintenance of essential services (see below) has been regarded as recognizing a right of employees to strike. This lack of a legislative framework is evidenced in the absence of regulation over forms of industrial action, including notice to strike, or on picketing. Sympathy strikes are rare. There are, however, some restrictions on the right to strike in some key sectors of the economy – for example, ports – on the grounds that strike action would harm the national interest by restricting essential services.

The individual contract of employment is suspended, not terminated, by strike action: once work resumes continuity of employment is guaranteed. Theoretically an employer could dismiss strikers, except those (in the main employee representative bodies) who enjoy special protection against dismissal. However, the employees would still be entitled to due notice, or payment in lieu.

Because trade unions have no legal personality and have been sufficiently powerful to resist all past attempts to have it conferred on them, they cannot be sued, nor can an employer take out an injunction against them to prevent or stop strike action, even if it might entail breaching a peace clause in a collective agreement.

Since the late 1980s there has been some court intervention in the area of industrial action. For example, strikers were injuncted for impeding the passage of goods into a factory on the grounds that third-party rights had been violated. An injunction might also be granted on the grounds that a strike could lead to irreparable damage to an enterprise. However, this kind of legal action is infrequent. Lock-outs are not specifically unlawful, unless intended to attack trade union organization as such, but are rare.

Each union is bound by its own rules in declaring a strike. Normally an internal ballot is conducted in which a majority, often two-thirds, must support the action. Unions exercise strict internal discipline; wildcat strikes are infrequent and when they do occur are often initiated by non-unionists. Collective agreements usually include a period of notice, often seven days, of strike action, as well as including conciliation procedures.

Industrial conflict is typically characterized by short disputes, the form of which is unregulated, which are aimed at disruption rather than a protracted contest. Employee reluctance to engage in prolonged disputes is also prompted by the loss of a number of bonuses.

Collective dismissal

The EC directive on collective dismissal has been implemented by two national collective agreements, No. 10 and No. 24, concluded in the National Labour Council and by a royal decree of 24 May 1976. In establishments with twenty or more employees the employer must inform the works council (or if one does not exist, the trade union delegation) in writing of the intention to declare redundancies. Collective dismissal is defined as dismissal taking place over sixty days involving:

- Ten workers from a work force of between twenty and 100.
- Ten per cent of a work force of between 100 and 300 employees.
- Thirty employees in establishments with more than 300 employees.

The information supplied to employee representatives must state the reason for the dismissals, the number of workers likely to be affected, the period over which redundancies will take place, and average number of workers employed.

Employers must also inform the National Employment Office (ONEm) of details of the redundancies. The information must include:

- Details of the company (including the numbers employed).
- The joint committee covering the company.
- The reasons for the redundancies.
- The numbers to be made redundant, by sex, age, occupation and department.
- Details of consultations held with employee representatives.

Employee representatives may also submit their views to ONEm. No formal notice of redundancy may be issued to any employee until thirty days have elapsed from the time of official notification. ONEm may shorten this period or lengthen it to sixty days. However, no official authorization of the redundancies as such is required, and the employer can proceed once the required waiting period has elapsed.

Periods of notice are as required in the case of individual dismissal. An employer who fails to give proper notice becomes liable to pay compensation equal to the notice period. Under the Contracts of Employment Act 1978 (articles 59, 60) employers must observe a minimum period of notice for *blue-collar* employees as follows:

- Not less than seven days, for workers with less than six months' service, and twenty-eight days for those with up to twenty years' service.
- Fifty-six days for those with twenty-plus years' service.

Under collective agreements employers often have to give more generous notice. The steel and metalworking industry agreements specify that blue-collar workers must be given twenty-eight days' notice if they have less than ten years' service, fifty-six days (between ten and twenty years') and 112 days (over twenty years').

The Contracts of Employment Act (articles 82 and 83) specifies that *white-collar* employees paid less than Bf 766,000 a year (£12,800) are entitled to:

- At least three months' notice for less than five years' service.
- Six months' for between five and ten years' service.
- Nine months' for between ten and fifteen years' service.
- Twelve months' for fifteen to twenty years' service.
- Fifteen months' for twenty to twenty-five years' service, with a further three months' for each additional five years' service.

(More details of periods of notice can be found in the second volume of the European Management Guides series, *Terms and Conditions of Employment*.)

Employees are entitled to pay for the period of notice, together with a special payment in the event of collective redundancy (*indemnité due en cas de licenciement collectif*). This is payable by the employer to employees for four months after employment ends, with reductions for employees whose notice period is longer than three months. The payment is equivalent to 50 per cent of the difference between unemployment benefit and previous net salary up to an annually revised ceiling. Additional payments may also be negotiated under redundancy schemes agreed at company level.

Closure

Procedures for notification and payments in the event of closure are set out in a law of 28 June 1966. Should the work force of a company fall below a quarter of that employed in the preceding year as a result of a cessation of a business or part of a business, the company must inform:

- The work force.
- Employee representatives.
- The Ministry of Labour and the Ministry of Economic Affairs.
- The National Employment Office.
- The 'closure fund' responsible for payments to employees.
- The appropriate joint committee.

Special payments are due in the event of a closure, although employees do not receive them as well as normal collective redundancy payments.

Transfer of undertakings

Transfer of undertakings is regulated by national agreement No. 32 *bis*. Employers have to respect existing contracts when a business is transferred, either totally or partially. Transfer in itself cannot constitute a reason for redundancy, either for the previous or the new owner. The establishment's works council, health and safety committee and trade union delegation stay in place and operate as normal.

Appendix

National Employment Office
(ONEm):
boulevard de l'Empereur 7
1000 Brussels
tel. + 32 2 510 2011
(French-speakers)
+ 32 2 513 8942
(Flemish-speakers)

Ministry of Labour:
rue Belliard 53
1040 Brussels
tel. +32 2 230 9010

Collective Industrial Relations
Service (for copies of
industry/sectoral collective
agreements):
rue Belliard 51
1040 Brussels
tel. + 32 2 233 4149

Conseil National du Travail
(for copies of national
collective agreements):
avenue de la Joyeuse Entrée 17–21
1040 Brussels
tel. + 32 2 233 8811

Federation of Belgian Enterprises
(Fédération des Entreprises de
Belgique, FEB; Verbond van
Belgische Ondernemingen, VBO)
rue Ravenstein 4
1000 Brussels
tel. + 32 2 515 0811

General Confederation of Belgian
Labour (Fédération
Générale du Travail de
Belgique, FGTB; Algemeen
Belgisch Vakverbond, ABVV):
rue Haute 42
1000 Brussels
tel. + 32 2 511 6466

Confederation of Christian
Trade Unions (Confédération
des Syndicats Chrétiens de
Belgique, CSC; Algemeen
Christelijk
Vakverbond, ACV):
rue de la Loi 121
1040 Brussels
tel. + 32 2 237 3676

Note
In order to simplify the text, references to institutions or terms have been
rendered only in French; the Flemish names for organizations are set out
above. However, linguistic sensibilities are an important consideration for
firms operating in Belgium.

2
Denmark

Industrial relations in Denmark are extensively based on collective agreements, including central agreements setting a basic framework for industrial relations conduct. Union membership is very high, and procedures for employee participation are largely based on institutions agreed with and operated through the trade unions. Despite the priority accorded to collective bargaining, the government has been prepared to intervene directly on a variety of issues, including forced conciliation to end strike action.

National-level consultation and co-operation

Denmark possesses a tripartite national Economic Council (*Økonomiske Råd*), established in 1962, which reports to the government on economic issues. Trade unions are represented by two centres, LO and FTF (see below) which regard the council as a valuable forum for discussing national economic developments. Danish trade unions also participate in the Council of Nordic Trade Unions (NFS). The NFS both advises and lobbies the Nordic Council of Ministers and the Nordic Council.

During the 1980s there were tripartite negotiations and consultation on a number of issues, although relations between the trade unions and the Conservative-led coalition government were at times severely strained. In 1984, for example, the LO union confederation pulled out of tripartite discussions on whether and how to implement cuts in working hours after accusing the government of taking the employers' side: a report produced by the Ministry of Labour on the issue at the request of the trade unions identified a number of criteria which had to be met before shorter hours could be introduced, which the employers claimed could not be met. The government eventually intervened directly to end strikes over the LO claim for shorter hours, in March 1985.

In the mid to late 1980s tripartite discussions took place

around models of profit-sharing, although no specific proposals emerged; on the implications of an ILO ruling which had found against the government's suspension of pay indexation; and, in 1987, on measures to contain wage costs through a reduction in employers' overall social insurance contributions, which were cut to approximately 5 per cent of employees' pay. In 1988 discussions centred on trade union demands for supplementary occupational (*Arbejdsmarkedspensioner*) pensions, which have subsequently been progressively introduced via collective bargaining. More recently attention has been directed at the structural problems of the Danish labour market.

Central bipartite consultation and bargaining on fundamental principles and structures of industrial relations takes place between the main trade union centre, the Federation of Trade Unions (*Landsorganisation*, LO) and the Danish Employers' Confederation (*Dansk Arbejdsgiverforening*, DA), and is embodied in two core agreements. The General Agreement (*Hovedaftalen*) regulates each party's rights of organization and association, the recognition of managerial prerogatives, the status of collective agreements (see below), unfair dismissal, and enabling provisions – to be fleshed out by industry agreements – on shop stewards. The Co-operation Agreement (*Samarbejdsaftalen*), the main provisions of which are set out in the section on employee representation below, establishes a framework for industrial co-operation, information and consultation on a wide range of issues.

Collective bargaining on pay and conditions of employment in the private sector is the responsibility of individual sectoral or occupational trade unions and industry employers' organizations, based on framework agreements on procedures, and in the past on basic terms, arrived at centrally between the DA and LO.

Co-operation Board. Under the Co-operation Agreement, which regulates the setting up of co-operation committees (see below), the DA and LO have established a jointly financed Co-operation Board charged with promoting co-operation between managements and employees, assisting in instituting co-operation committees, and settling any disputes which may arise out of the operation of co-operation committees: the procedures here are dealt with in the following section.

Employee representation in the workplace

There are three forms of employee representation at workplace level: via shop stewards, through co-operation committees, with the two structures closely related, and through health and safety committees. Only health and safety committees are regulated by statute law. However, as noted above, the underlying collective agreements which provide for shop steward and co-operation committee rights are central and therefore binding throughout the private sector, subject to size criteria. There is no statutory form of employee representation comparable with the works councils found elsewhere in the European Community.

Shop stewards (Tillidsrepræsentant)

There is a long tradition of workplace representation via trade union shop stewards in Denmark, with agreed provisions on their election, status and role. Through national framework agreements, fleshed out by industry agreements, such provisions now cover most of the private sector. There is no statutory provision in this area. Section 8 of the General Agreement (see below) – which sets out the general agreed principles for the conduct of industrial relations – provides that industry agreements should make provision for shop stewards to be elected and recognized, unless the nature of the activity renders it impossible. Industry agreements prescribe detailed regulations on the election of shop stewards, and their specific rights and duties. On average there is one shop steward for every fifty employees, precise arrangements depending on the structure of the individual enterprise.

The minimum conditions for candidacy as a shop steward typically include:

- *Union membership* – as the shop steward serves as the local/workplace representative of a trade union.
- *Length of service.* Normally a year's seniority is required, reflecting the requirement that the shop steward should have a sound knowledge of the undertaking.
- *Recognition as a 'capable worker'.* Shop stewards must be acknowledged as a 'capable worker' (*anerkendt dygtig medarbejder*), although this may be interpreted broadly. The reason

lies in the special protection against dismissal enjoyed by shop stewards, giving the employer a legitimate interest in having only capable employees in this especially secure position. Should an employer contest the election of a shop steward, the onus rests with the employer to show that the candidate does not meet the requirement.

In larger companies with many stewards, the stewards may establish a joint union delegation. Agreements also provide for the establishment of trade union 'clubs' in larger organizations, which can embrace members of several trade unions who elect a common shop steward. Under industry agreements, employers may be required to provide facilities for 'club' meetings.

Collective agreements often require that, as the representative of the work force *vis-á-vis* the employer as well as the workplace representative of the trade union, shop stewards, once elected, must be approved in office by the relevant union, and the employer informed.

Shop stewards serve as a direct link between employees and management on issues relating to workplace terms and conditions, and as such figure as the central channel through which employee grievances are articulated, although collective agreements generally state that relations between the parties should be co-operative rather than confrontational. For example, the agreement covering clerical employees states that; 'it is incumbent upon the shop steward to behave with diligence towards colleagues, the organisation [i.e. the trade union] and the employer, to seek to resolve conflicts and to maintain industrial co-operation at the workplace'.

Collective agreements also establish grievance procedures, speci-fying the stage at which individual problems may be referred to stewards, and at what point a grievance can be taken to the relevant trade union.

Shop stewards customarily enjoy time-off rights to carry out their activities, although specific amounts of time are not usually set out.

As a rule, collective agreements contain special provisions pro-tecting shop stewards against dismissal. In general, a shop steward can be dismissed only when the employer has 'compelling grounds', such as serious misconduct.

Co-operation committees

'Co-operation committees' have existed in the private sector since the immediate post-war period and function under a central collective agreement negotiated between the DA and LO: the most recent agreement dates from 1986. There are an estimated 3,000 such committees in the private sector. Co-operation committees are envisaged as a means of furthering employee participation and industrial co-operation with the objective of promoting 'competitiveness and employee job satisfaction'. The preamble to the Co-operation Agreement stresses the importance of 'motivating management systems' and 'active participation by employees and their elected union representatives', with particular emphasis on the need for management, co-operation and communication systems to 'induce as many employees as possible to participate in arranging and organizing their daily work'.

Co-operation committees may be set up in enterprises with thirty-five or more employees, and may be proposed either by the employer or by a majority of employees. The Co-operation Agreement recommends 'informative meetings' between management and employees 'at frequent intervals' should neither side wish to establish a formal co-operation committee. The committee consists of managers and senior personnel ineligible for trade union membership on the one hand, and on the other of all the rest of the employees in the enterprise. The size of the committee varies according to the size of the company, ranging from two representatives from each side for enterprises with thirty-five to fifty employees up to six from each side for enterprises with over 500 employees. Election of employee representatives to the committee, which takes place every two years, is by direct vote of the whole work force.

Elected shop stewards are *ex officio* members of the co-operation committee. Should the number of stewards exceed the number of places available on the committee, election is solely from among the stewards. Committee members, like shop stewards, enjoy protection from dismissal in the form of an extended period of notice of six weeks in addition to their contractual notice.

The co-operation committee is chaired by a senior manager, with the employees nominating the deputy chair. Meetings must be held six times a year, unless an individual local agreement makes a different provision.

Co-operation committees have the following rights and duties (Co-operation Agreement, 1986, section 3):

- Establishing principles for the work environment and human relations, as well as principles for the personnel policy pursued by the enterprise towards the employees represented in the staff group of the co-operation committee.
- Establishing the principles of training and retraining for employees who are to work with new technology.
- Establishing principles for the in-house compilation, storage and use of personal data.
- Exchanging views and considering proposals for guidelines on the planning of production and work, and the implementation of major changes in the enterprise.
- Assessing the technical, financial, staffing, educational and environmental consequences of the introduction of new technology and major changes to existing technology.
- Informing employees about proposals for incentive systems of payment, including details of their basis, structure, effect and application. Also informing employees about the possibility of setting up funds for educational and social security purposes.

Under the 1986 agreement any employees displaced through the introduction of new technology have a right to up to four weeks' time off to attend retraining and reorientation courses, with the employer covering loss of pay and course fees for any employee with at least a year's service.

Employers are required to inform the committee, 'in plain language' and in good time, of the firm's financial position and future prospects, the employment outlook, and any major changes contemplated, including the application of new technology. The information disclosed must not harm the employer's interests, and the committee may be bound to secrecy on some issues. The committee, in turn, is obliged to develop appropriate means for communicating information to the work force.

Co-operation committees are not empowered to deal with issues which are in the province of collective bargaining proper – that is, industry or company pay matters.

Disputes arising out of the operation of co-operation committees, if irresolvable at company level, may be taken to the Co-operation

Board set up under the national agreement. If discussion at this level is unable to settle the dispute, then an arbitrator may be appointed – if necessary, by the president of the Labour Court.

Health and safety representatives and committees

Under the 1985 Health and Safety at Work Act, originally passed in 1975, employees in companies with a work force of at least ten people must elect a safety representative who, together with a supervisor, constitutes a safety group for the enterprise. In companies with at least twenty employees a safety committee (*Sikkerhedsudvalg*) must be set up to ensure that working conditions are in accordance with the relevant regulations. Inspectors from the Health and Safety Executive (*Arbejdstilsynet*) must make regular contact with safety representatives and members from the committee. Safety representatives – as well as other employees – are free to discuss issues relating to health and safety at the workplace with the executive.

Safety representatives have a right to time off and, like shop stewards, are protected against certain types of dismissal.

Employee representation at board level

Provision for board-level representation was introduced by the 1974 Companies Act, amended in 1980. All limited liability companies and companies limited by guarantee are required to establish a two-tier board structure, with a supervisory board and a management board. While the management board is concerned with day-to-day operations, the supervisory board – which must consist of at least three members – is responsible for overall policy, and must be consulted on important decisions. Secondary legislation specifies the regulations on employee representation at board level.

In companies which have employed at least thirty-five workers over the previous three years, employees have a legal right to vote on whether to elect employee representatives. Any employee who is of age and has at least a year's service is eligible. Employees may elect at least two, and up to half the number, of the shareholder representatives elected by the shareholders' meeting. Employee representatives have the same rights and duties as other board members, are elected for four years, and have the same entitlement to dismissal protection as shop stewards. The supervisory board must ensure that employees are given information on the circumstances of the company, including finances, employment, and production plans.

Trade unions

Trade union structure

Three union centres, the LO, FTF and AC, organize a total of some 2·1 million employees, approximately 80–5 per cent of the work force.

The LO (Landsorganisation), which is closely aligned with the Social Democratic Party, is the largest, representing over 1·4 million employees in twenty-nine individual unions. Around one-third of the LO's membership is in private companies affiliated to the employers' confederation, the DA. The organizing principles of the constituent unions vary. The most significant are:

- The National Union of Commercial and Clerical Workers (HK), with some 320,000 members in both the public and the private sectors.
- The National Union of General Workers (SID), with some 313,000 throughout industry, transport and in agriculture.
- The National Union of Metalworkers, with 140,000 members.
- The National Union of Women Workers, with 100,000 members.

The LO is currently attempting to rationalize its representation by establishing seven basic sectoral 'cartels', so that union members with the same employer would be in the same cartel. An experimental period, lasting until 1995, has been designated to try out the new arrangements, which are, as yet, proving problematic. Some rationalization in the overall number of trade unions has taken place, from fifty-six in 1970 to twenty-nine in 1990. The LO itself is competent to bargain, a right delegated to it by the constituent unions, and its role goes beyond that of co-ordinating or mediating between its affiliates. As noted above, the LO and DA have concluded wide-ranging central agreements establishing the basic principles for the conduct of industrial relations as well as regulating matters such as unfair dismissal procedures. The extent to which bargaining over pay and other terms is conducted centrally by the LO or predominantly by the individual unions has varied from time to time, with the most recent past since 1987 dominated by decentralized bargaining on pay against the background of a central four-year agreement on hours.

The FTF union, which represents some 350,000 white-collar employees and civil servants, is not affiliated to the LO and was established in 1952 as a politically neutral trade union.

The AC, the Confederation of Professional Associations, was established via a merger of several professional organizations in 1972 and has approximately 140,000 members.

Although initially regarded as a competitor of the LO, the FTF has been recognized by the Social Democratic Party, and since 1972 has had an agreement with the LO for mutual recognition and to prevent inter-union competition. All three union centres customarily present common demands to employers.

The right to organize

Complementary to the constitutionally guaranteed right to form associations for any legal purpose, section 1 of the General Agreement between the DA and LO provides that the two organizations 'undertake not to hinder employers and workers, either directly or indirectly, in organizing themselves within the organizational framework of the central organizations. It is considered to be an anti-organization act if one of the parties . . . acts against another party because of organizational affiliation rather than industrial issues'. Employers, for example, may not therefore discriminate against unionized employees by refusing to employ them.

Closed shops are valid in the private sector. Although DA prohibits affiliated companies from entering into closed shop agreements without special permission, employers not in DA – who employ one-third of the LO's membership – often do so. As a consequence of the British Rail judgement in the European Court of Human Rights in 1981, the Danish parliament passed legislation providing for protection in the event of dismissal both for being and for not being a member of a trade union. Accordingly, an employer may not dismiss an employee for not being a union member unless the employee knew that union membership was a condition of employment.

Employers' organizations

The largest and most significant private-sector employer organization is the DA (*Dansk Arbejdsgiverforening*), with a membership of some 30,000 companies organized into fifty industrial groupings which DA hopes to rationalize down to ten. The largest are the Danish Industries Employers' Association (IA), the Employers' Association for Trade Transport and Services (AHTS), the Employers' Association for the Shop and Office Sectors (BKA) and the Employers' Association for the Construction Industry (ByG). Although the DA organizes only employers covering around 500,000 workers, its agreements with the LO – around 600 in all – serve as pace-setters for bargaining elsewhere in the economy. As with the LO, and depending on the issue or overall policy direction, agreements may be centrally concluded or left to constituent associations.

Apart from the DA, there are two other major employers' associations in the private sector: the Employers' Association for the Financial Sector (FA) and SALA, the Confederation of Danish Agricultural Enterprises.

Bargaining

Danish industrial relations are characterized by free collective bargaining, with a major role allotted to collective agreements in areas typically regulated by statute in other European Community countries. However, the state has a conciliation service which can intervene in disputes and did so in the 1980s – most notably during the dispute over shorter working hours in March 1985. In the early 1980s there was also a four-year pay policy introduced by the Conservative-led coalition government which suspended the pay indexation system. (Pay determination and pay bargaining will be dealt with specifically in the fourth volume of the European Management Guides series.)

Based on the framework General and Co-operation Agreements already referred to above, most bargaining on terms and conditions of employment in the private sector is carried out by the individual unions and industrial employers' associations.

Collective agreements are normally concluded every other year, with most private-sector agreements expiring on 1 March. The recent four-year agreement contained a mid-term reopener clause. Collective agreements bind signatory organizations, and the terms must be applied by signatory employers to all employees, whether unionized or not. Agreements typically include a 'peace clause' (*Fredspligt*) outlawing industrial action during the lifetime of an agreement, save for exceptional circumstances set out in the so-called Standard Rules for Handling Labour Disputes (see below) agreed in 1908: these include situations where there is a risk 'to life, welfare or honour' (see below, 'Industrial action').

All collective agreements must be ratified by union members in a ballot before they can be signed and put into effect by the negotiating parties.

Conciliation machinery

The Standard Rules commit the parties to seek to resolve disputes by mediation or, if necessary, by arbitration. If one of the parties requests it, mediation must take place within a maximum of five working days. Should mediation fail, the matter is initially referred back to the negotiating parties for further talks.

If the dispute concerns the interpretation of an existing agreement ('dispute over rights'), the matter may be submitted to a court of arbitration if one of the parties requests it: if a party refuses on the grounds that the dispute is one of interests – for example, over the terms of a new agreement – then the validity of the refusal can be referred to the Labour Court, which includes representatives of both sides of industry. Where the dispute concerns an alleged breach of an agreement, the issue will be dealt with directly by the Labour Court.

Disputes over interests during negotiations can be referred to the state Conciliation Board established by the Ministry of Labour. Preliminary notice of industrial action (strike or lock-out) can be given if no agreement is reached after negotiations involving the Conciliation Board: the conciliator can postpone industrial action twice, each time for fourteen days.

Industrial action

In principle employers and employees both have a right to resort to industrial action, subject to the constraints imposed by agreements, such as the peace obligations noted above, and partly also by law. The General Agreement concluded between the DA and LO also provides that no stoppage of work may take place 'unless approved by at least three-quarters of the votes cast by a competent assembly under the rules of the relevant organization and unless due notice has been given to the other party'. The executive committees of the DA and LO have to be informed of any intention to stop work at least fourteen days before the proposed stoppage, and the other party must be given seven days' notice.

The Labour Court may fine anyone engaged in unofficial strike action, or other action which breaches the General Agreement. Following a case before the court in 1989, the standardized fines in force were raised to Dkr 32 per hour (£2.82) for skilled workers and Dkr 27 per hour (£2.32) for unskilled workers. Action may not be proceeded with if the central organizations jointly meet to resolve the problem and those engaged in the action resume work immediately. Unions can be fined if they fail to use all reasonable means to prevent an unlawful stoppage.

Collective dismissal

Collective dismissals are regulated by an Amendment to the Act on Labour Exchange Activity and Unemployment Benefits, which gives effect to the 1975 EC directive.

The provisions apply where the following numbers of persons are to be made redundant within a period of thirty days:

- At least ten in undertakings which normally employ more than twenty and fewer than 100 workers.
- At least 10 per cent of the work force in undertakings which normally employ at least 100 but fewer than 300 workers.
- At least thirty in undertakings which normally employ at least 300 workers.

An employer wishing to effect redundancies on this scale must inform the work force in writing at least thirty days before notice is to be issued. Arrangements must be made as quickly as possible to discuss with employee representatives ways of avoiding or reducing the number of redundancies and of mitigating their consequences. The employer must inform the work force of the grounds for the redundancies, the number of workers affected, and the period over which redundancies will be effected.

If no means can be found of averting the dismissals, the employer must inform the Labour Market Board (*Arbejdsmarkedsnævnet*), giving the names of employees scheduled for redundancy. Employee representatives can append their own observations to the employer's notification. Redundancies can proceed only thirty days after the board has been notified, provided that the board does not decide to shorten or lengthen the period.

Failure to comply with the law could make the employer liable to a fine and compensation to employees equal to the thirty days required for notification.

Periods of notice are as for individual termination, with considerable variation, depending on the category of employee and length of service. There is a major difference in provision for white-collar and blue-collar employees. For termination by the employer of a white-collar employee's employment, the Salaried Employees Act provides that the employer should give at least:

- One month's notice, to expire at the end of the month, during the first six months of employment.
- Three months' notice, to expire at the end of a month, after six months of employment.
- The period of notice above shall be increased by one month for every three years of service, subject to a maximum of six months.

Blue-collar workers are entitled to two to three weeks' notice after one year's employment and four to seven weeks' notice after two to three years' employment. Long-service employees, with ten to twelve years' service, may be entitled to up to three or four months' notice.

There are no provisions for statutory or agreed redundancy payments. Employees receive pay for notice, and in the case of white-collar workers any service-related severance pay (see the second volume of the European Management Guides series, on conditions of employment).

Transfer of undertakings

EC directive 77/187 on acquired rights has been implemented in Denmark through the Employee Rights on the Transfer of Undertakings Act, 1979. Employers must inform employee representatives in good time of the reasons for the transfer, its economic and social effects, and measures to be taken to safeguard workers' interests. The transferee assumes the rights and obligations of the former employer, and specifically any collectively agreed provisions and individual terms of employment.

Termination of employment on grounds of transfer of ownership would constitute wrongful dismissal unless the dismissal were due to economic or technical factors which necessitated a reorganization of the work force. The employer must, if necessary, demonstrate that the presumption of wrongful dismissal is incorrect.

Appendix

Ministry of Labour
International Section:
19 Laksegade
1063 Copenhagen K
tel. + 45 33 92 59 00

Arbejdsmarkedsstyrelsen
(National Labour Market
Authority)
Adelgade 13
1304 Copenhagen K
tel. + 45 38 17 20 00

Dansk Arbejdsgiverforening
(Danish Employers' Federation):
Vester Voldgade 113
1790 Copenhagen V
(publishes a guide to employment
in Denmark in English)
tel. + 45 33 93 40 00
fax + 45 33 12 29 76

Landsorganisation (Danish
Confederation of Trade Unions)
Rosenørns Allé 12
1634 Copenhagen V
tel. + 45 31 35 35 41
fax + 45 35 37 37 41

Dansk Metalarbejderforbund
(National Metalworkers' Union):
Nyropsgade 38
1602 Copenhagen V
tel. + 45 33 12 82 12

3

France

Trade union density in France is amongst the lowest in Europe and has fallen markedly since the late 1970s. However, trade union representatives remain the main force behind statutory workplace participation; such mechanisms often fail to function at all in sectors with very low union membership. The law provides principally for information and consultation rights at establishment level, with effective employee decision-making confined to the organization of cultural activities.

The 1980s saw the growth of employer-led structures of employee involvement, paralleling and often supplanting statutory structures because of the greater resources devoted by employers to making them function, and their perceived greater relevance to employees' working life compared with the 'rights of expression' conferred by the law. From being traditionally underdeveloped, workplace collective bargaining has been fostered by legislation, passed in 1982, which requires employers to negotiate annually with workforce representatives.

Co-operation at national level

There is no institutionalized form of tripartite bargaining in France. However, there is a tripartite forum, the National Collective Bargaining Board, which consists of representatives of the central employer's organization, the trade union centres and the government: its main task is to review legislation related to collective agreements and to decide on increases in SMIC, the minimum wage. Bipartite consultation does not take place through an institutional forum as such. Nevertheless, the main employers' organization, the CNPF, and the main union confederations have met regularly at national level in recent years. The two parties set a broad agenda in the late 1980s, with the focus of talks on working time flexibility, sex equality and training. Negotiations have generally resulted in a multi-industry agreement (*accord interprofessionel*) which is not itself legally binding but which serves to provide a framework within which collective and company agreements can be drawn up. For example, current talks on an agreement on training aim to establish guidelines on how often employers and employees should meet to discuss training provision and strategy. These national agreements have also served as a forum for airing topics on which new legislation is planned, and agreements may precede a new law. For example, legislation is expected to follow the training agreement once it is finalized.

The Economic and Social Council (*Conseil Economique et Sociale*) is a research and advisory body which publishes reports on economic and social policy. Its members include employee organizations, business representatives, the professions and individuals engaged in social activities such as housing associations.

Workplace employee participation

Employee participation in France (*représentation du personnel*) is determined largely by statutory provisions which require represent-ative bodies to be elected at establishment or company level. Trade union representation in the workplace is also regulated by law (see below, 'Trade unions'). Workplace representative bodies do not negotiate or conclude collective agreements: this is solely the prerogative of trade unions. The type and size of representative organization required depends on the size of the undertaking. In undertakings with eleven to forty-nine employees, staff representatives (*délégués du personnel*) must be elected; undertakings with fifty or more employees are required to have works committees (*comités d'entreprise*). Staff representatives or works committees may also be established in smaller companies than those specified by law under a collective agreement.

Staff representatives (*délégués du personnel*)

Under legislation dating from 1936, there is a statutory obligation for staff representatives to be elected in public and private undertakings with at least eleven employees. (Companies with

fewer than eleven employees may do so by collective or house
agreement if desired.) The responsibility for ensuring that the
law is complied with rests with the employer. The number of
representatives to be elected depends on the size of the work force,
ranging from one representative and one deputy in companies of
eleven to twenty-five employees to ten representatives and ten
deputies in companies of 1,000 employees, with a further one
representative and one deputy for each further 250 employees.

All employees are eligible to be elected as staff representatives
provided that they are not related to the employer, are above
eighteen years of age, speak French and have at least one
year's service in the company. Staff representatives are elected
for a one-year renewable mandate; if there is more than one
representative they are divided equally between two categories
(blue and white-collar workers and technicians and supervisory
staff). Election is by secret ballot on lists of candidates proposed in
the first instance by the trade unions represented at the workplace.
Should the number of votes cast be fewer than half the total number
of eligible votes, then a second round must be held within fifteen
days. Independent candidates are entitled to stand in the second
round. This rarely happens in practice and the vast majority of staff
representatives are trade union nominees.

The 1982 legislation also provides for the election of inter-
company staff representatives where several undertakings with
fewer than eleven employees operate on a single site, provided there
are at least fifty employees in all on the site and the undertakings
are likely to experience common difficulties connected with the
working environment. This may be the case on a building site, a
business centre or a shopping centre. The local labour inspector
may enforce this regulation if deemed appropriate or if trade union
sections request it.

Duties and rights of staff representatives. Staff representatives are
empowered to represent employees' interests to the employer,
individually or collectively, on matters concerning the Labour
Code, social protection, health and safety and any matters covered
in a company or relevant industry collective agreement. They may
also raise individual or collective pay grievances but do not bargain
on pay as such: wage bargaining is conducted between the employer
and trade union representatives (see below). Employees also have

the right to go direct to the employer with a grievance if they so wish.

Staff representatives must be consulted by the employer on matters relating to length of holidays and holiday planning, health and safety matters, redundancy and reclassification of employees following an industrial accident. Staff representatives also communicate with other employee representative bodies if they exist, such as works committees and health and safety committees.

If no works committee exists in a company, that is, if the company employs fewer than fifty people or no works committee has been set up through lack of candidates, then staff representatives must be informed by the employer on matters such as the general economic and financial situation of the company, the introduction of new technology, changes in working conditions, and training.

Status of staff representatives. Staff representatives have the right to fifteen hours' a month paid time off to carry out their duties, in addition to time spent at meetings. This number of hours may be increased in exceptional circumstances. If there is no works committee, it is increased to twenty hours a month. Staff representatives have the right to meet the employer at least once a month and can request additional meetings, which the employer cannot refuse. If there is a works committee, as well as staff representatives, the employer must arrange separate meetings. If employers wilfully hinder the election or functioning of employee representation they can be charged in court (*délit d'entrave*) and can face a prison sentence of two months – two years and/or a fine of F 2,000–40,000 (£190–3,800).

Staff representatives also enjoy protection against dismissal, except for gross misconduct (*faute grave*) during the whole of their term of office (Labour Code, articles L 425–1–3). Candidates for election as staff representative enjoy protection against dismissal for six months from the publication of the list of candidates. Former representatives are protected for six months following the expiry of their term.

According to a Ministry of Labour survey, published in 1990, the number of staff representatives in companies surveyed declined by 5 per cent between 1985 and 1988. An estimated 57 per cent of companies in 1988 which should have had staff representatives in place were found to have none, compared with 52 per cent in

1985. In the Ministry's view, this may have been due in part to the general decline of trade union membership lowering the pool and motivation of potential candidates, even though independent candidates may stand. Moreover, the number of large companies with traditionally strong union representation has also fallen in recent years. The growing influence of 'Japanese' industrial relations practices, in which direct contact between employees and managers has supplanted or overshadowed representative structures, is also felt to have played an important role in the 1980s. Low rates of staff representation appear to be typical in small and medium-size companies (eleven to forty-nine employees): larger companies show a much higher rate of compliance with the law. For example, 78 per cent of companies with 100–499 employees and 98 per cent of larger companies had staff representatives.

Works committees (*comités d'entreprise*)

Under legislation passed in 1946, and amended in 1975 and 1982, the election of works committees is obligatory in companies employing fifty or more staff (Labour Code, article 431–1) and is voluntary in smaller companies. Works committees can be elected at three different levels – group (*groupe*), undertaking (*entreprise*) and establishment (*établissement*) – if the company is large enough to employ more than fifty people at all three levels. In practice, however, as a Ministry of Labour survey discovered, some 18 per cent of companies employing fifty to ninety-nine staff had no works committees in place. According to the Ministry survey, this was mainly due to a lack of candidates. It also found that works committees in small and medium-size companies do not carry out all their statutory functions, some concentrating wholly on the administration of cultural activities. Only 30 per cent of companies surveyed were informing works committees fully, in line with the law, and 25 per cent of all committees received no information at all from their employer. Consultation took place regularly in 10–15 per cent of committees.

Works committees are bipartite bodies and consist of the employer or their representative, who chairs the committee, elected employee delegates and trade union representatives if there are any (see below). Any nationally recognized trade union is entitled to elect a member to sit on the works committee as an observer. The number of elected employee representatives varies according to the number of employees in the company, ranging from three in companies of fifty to seventy-four employees to fifteen in companies of over 10,000 employees. This number may be modified by collective agreement. Each councillor has an elected deputy. Works committees are funded by the employer by a minimum annual amount equal to 0·2 per cent of the gross wage bill. Larger companies may devote a larger amount of the payroll to financing works committees. This money finances travelling expenses for committee members, all relevant and necessary documentation, and social and cultural activities for employees. The works committee has a free hand in managing the social and cultural activities budget.

Committee members are elected for a mandate of two years, which is renewable. Eligibility is the same as for staff representatives (see above).

Depending on the size of the undertaking, sub-committees must be created to deal with specific topics. For example, a vocational training committee (*commission de la formation professionelle*) must be set up in companies employing 200 or more staff, a housing committee (*commission d'information et d'aide au logement*) in companies employing 300 or more staff, and an economic committee (*commission économique*) in companies employing 1,000 or more staff.

Functions of the works committee. Works committees exist as an organ for the collective representation of employees on issues relating to pay, working conditions, training, and changes in working practices or working time. They enjoy various rights to consultation and information which the employer must respect (see below). There are a limited number of matters on which the employer must obtain the agreement of the works committee:

- The hiring or dismissal of a company doctor.
- The conclusion of a profit-sharing agreement.
- The institution of a four-day week or reorganization of individual working time.
- The formation of a health and safety committee.

However, in other circumstances, and except in the case of

organizing social and cultural activities, where it manages its own budget, their role is essentially one of consultation and not negotiation. Works committees cannot directly affect management decisions, although it is possible that they may influence policy decisions in areas such as training. According to a survey carried out by the trade union CFDT, there is wide variation in employer practice towards works committees. Whereas some employers refuse any co-operation, others regard committees as a source of help and advice. In general, the survey concluded that most employers treat the works committee as a useful means of exchanging ideas and as a forum for discussion.

Works committees must be *consulted* by the employer before action can be taken on a number of issues, including changes to the structure of the work force, working time, working conditions, training, mergers and acquisitions, the introduction of new technology, changes in maximum overtime, the implementation of short-time working, dismissals and redundancies.

Works committees must be *informed* by the employer on matters such as the economic situation of the company, minimum and actual rates of pay, the structure of the work force, including the number of part-timers, disabled employees and those on temporary contracts, annual overtime provisions, improvements in production methods and sabbatical and other leave.

Works committees are also responsible for organizing company social and cultural activities and managing the budget for that purpose, the budget being based on expenses incurred the previous year. Legislation is currently under discussion which would oblige companies without works committees (employing under fifty staff) to finance social and cultural activities through a fund equal to 0·2 per cent of the wage bill.

Meetings between the works committee and the employer are held once a month or twice if the majority of works committee members wish it. Employers who refuse to meet the works committee risk being found to have wilfully hindered the functioning of employee representation (*délit d'entrave*) and may be subject to the penalties outlined above.

Rights of works committee members. Works committee members are entitled by law to twenty hours a month paid time off in order to carry out works committee duties (extra time off may be awarded under exceptional circumstances). Under the law of 28 October 1982, on initial election works committee are entitled to attend an economic training course (*formation économique*) lasting up to a maximum of five days at a recognized institution. As with staff representatives, works committee members enjoy protection against dismissal during their period of office and for a period of six months thereafter. Candidates for election to the works committee are protected against dismissal for a period of three months following the announcement of the list of candidates.

Health and safety committees

Under legislation passed on 23 December 1982 health and safety committees must be set up in companies employing fifty or more staff. These committees consist of the employer, or their representative, and an employee delegation, the size of which depends on the size of the company and ranges from three in companies of up to 199 employees to nine in companies of 1,500 or more employees. A proportion of the employee delegation must consist of supervisors (*agents de maîtrise*) or managers (*cadres*). All employees are eligible to sit on the health and safety committee; the term of office is two years and is renewable.

Rights and duties of the health and safety committee. Health and safety committees are enjoined to protect the health and safety of all employees at the workplace, to oversee and improve working conditions, and to ensure that all legal provisions are complied with. The committee has a right to consultation and information but has no funds of its own and cannot make decisions directly binding on the undertaking. Committees must be consulted before any decision is made regarding significant changes to health and safety at work, changes to work stations, methods of production, or any other matters affecting the health and safety of employees. Committees are entitled to appoint an expert to examine any situation it deems to pose a serious risk. Committees are also entitled to carry out their own regular inspections of the workplace. In the case of disagreements between the employer and the committee, the matter may be taken to the high court (*tribunal de grande instance*).

Employers must present the committee with written reports, at least once a year, on the general health and safety situation of the company, and on current measures, or steps that have been taken during the previous year, to improve health and safety at the workplace. The committee will then give its reactions to the report and can propose priorities in the order of tasks to be undertaken.

Members of health and safety committees must treat the information given to them by the employer with discretion and respect the confidentiality of information regarding production processes.

Status of health and safety committee members. Health and safety committee members in companies with 300 or more employees are entitled to attend an initial training course of a maximum of five days. Members are also entitled to time off of two to twenty hours a month, depending on the size of the company. Members are entitled to the same protection against dismissal as members of works committees.

Employee representation at board level

There is no statutory provision for employee representation at board level. However, under the decree of 21 October 1986, companies may provide for a number of employee representatives to sit on the board of directors (*conseil d'administration*) which should not be more than four (or five in a quoted company) or a number equal to a third of the number of board members. The maximum period of office is six years and is renewable.

'Right of expression'. The law of 4 August 1982 (one of the 'Auroux' laws, named after the then Labour Minister), amended on 3 January 1986, provides for a general right on the part of all employees in the public and private sectors to express their view (*droit d'expression*) concerning the content, conditions and organization of work. Individual employees may go straight to members of management with an opinion or problem, without having to go through the usual employee representation channels. However, the rights are essentially collective, and the legislation deliberately allots a great deal of scope for interpretation by employers' and employees' organizations. It stipulates that agreements on employees' right of expression should be concluded

between employers and representative trade unions if the company employs fifty or more staff and has a trade union delegate, or if it has fewer than fifty staff but has a trade union delegate provided for by collective agreement.

Such an agreement should contain information concerning measures to be taken to ensure freedom of expression within the company and set out the level, frequency and duration of self-expression meetings. All meetings and consultation should take place at the workplace and during paid working hours.

If no agreement has been concluded, the employer must consult staff representatives at least once a year on the general subject of the right of expression. If an agreement does exist, employers should assess the operation of the provisions with the trade unions once every three years.

A Ministry of Labour report published in 1985 showed that agreements concluded covered employees in 45 per cent of eligible companies, with the majority of agreements providing for meetings within the context of a particular unit, such as a department. In 1989 446 agreements on the right of expression were signed, compared with 194 in 1988. However, some studies question the success of such agreements and self-expression groups. An ILO study (see 'Selected further reading') indicated that such groups may founder if not given a specific and relevant brief. The study found that quality circles, which expanded in the mid-1980s, were often more favoured by both employees and management as they set out to tackle specific problems, often with a direct outcome for the individual's job, and were well supported by managements.

Trade unions

Trade union structure

Trade unions in France are general unions, with divisions – though not absolutely rigid ones – along political and religious lines. There are five employee confederations recognized as having representative status, of which one is a managerial association. They are (with membership figures as provided by the unions):

- Confédération Générale du Travail (CGT), with approximately 1·6 million members.

- Confédération Générale du Travail–Force Ouvrière (CGT–FO), with 1,150,000 members, established by non-communist members of the CGT in 1947.
- Confédération Française Démocratique du Travail (CFDT), with 950,000 members, originally a Christian trade union (CFTC) but which abandoned religious affiliation in 1964.
- Confédération Française des Travailleurs Chrétiens (CFTC), with 260,000 members, set up in 1965 by the Christian minority in the 'old' CFTC after the establishment of the CFDT.
- Confédération Générale des Cadres (CGC), the managers' union, with 325,000 members.

Each of the confederations has a number of industrial and occupational federations, including sections representing managers. Co-operation between the different unions is limited by differing political positions. The CGT has communist leanings and has a large representation among skilled manual workers in metalworking, chemicals, mining, steel and in the docks. It often refuses to sign collective agreements. The CGT–FO maintains that it has no political orientation, although it does profess to be anti-communist, and represents mainly white-collar workers, technicians, professional people and employees in the public sector. The CFDT has informal links with the socialist party and mainly represents employees in the health service, oil, metalworking and finance. The CFTC is guided by Catholic principles and has a large representation among teachers and miners. The CGC is a managerial union with a strong representation in metalworking and chemicals.

Low union density

Traditionally union density has never been high in France, and it has been steadily declining since the late 1970s, following a wave of redundancies and major company restructuring. Only around 10 per cent of the work force is estimated to be unionized. There are many reasons for the low level of union membership, rooted in both the political and the industrial orientation of the main unions, with an emphasis on the creation of an activist cadre rather than a mass membership, and the structure of French industry. The protection of employee rights by a written labour code and a substantial legal framework both reflects and compensates for weak union organization. At the same time, it does little to highlight the need or benefits of independent collective representation. Many employees, around half the work force, are employed in small companies where there is no union representation and where the culture militates against individual membership. Furthermore, under the system of extension of collective agreements across sectors, everybody benefits from an agreement, whether or not they belong to a trade union. The changing structure of the work force has also resulted in lower union membership; in the 1980s the work force became more skilled and educated, and the proportion of women employed rose. Traditional areas of unionization such as heavy industry and shipbuilding shrank, to be replaced by an enlarged tertiary sector.

Rights of association

The freedom to join a trade union (*la liberté syndicale*) is a constitutional right and is also provided for in the Labour Code, article L411–5: 'All employees, regardless of sex, age and nationality, are free to join the trade union of their choice'. Membership of a trade union should in no way influence any recruitment or dismissal decision on the part of an employer; employers must not include questions on such matters on application forms. Employees also have the right not to join a union: there is therefore no legal basis for the closed shop. Under the law of 28 October 1982 trade unions are 'organizations with a particular legal status, grouping individuals in the same or similar profession, having the sole object of defending the rights and material and moral interests of its members'. Trade unions are free to organize and meet as they wish. Unions may also set their own rules but when setting up must give a copy of their statute to the local government headquarters (*mairie*).

Trade union representation

Workers can be represented by trade unions at national, industry and company level. At national level, trade unions sit on the National Collective Bargaining Board and the Social and Economic Council; at industry level, at least one trade union must sign a collective agreement for it to be valid – trade unions that have not signed have the power to veto the extension of the agreement across a sector.

Trade union representation at the workplace

Legislation dating from 1982, and passed under the first Mitterrand presidency, set out to bolster the position of the trade unions at company level and encourage company-based collective bargaining. Under the (Auroux) law of 28 October 1982 every nationally represented trade union, such as the CGT, CFDT, CGT–FO, CFTC, CGC or any other union, has the right to set up a trade union section (*section syndicale*) in a company, regardless of the company's size, if it can prove that it is adequately represented within the company. The law stipulates that trade union sections should 'ensure the representation of the material and moral interests of employees'. Trade union sections are normally set up at company rather than plant level, unless it can be proven that the plant is of a separate character from the company as a whole. Trade union sections may appoint a representative to the company works committee, but this is not obligatory. The presence of a trade union section in a company obliges the employer to bargain annually on pay, working time, training and the right of expression. However, the obligation is only to negotiate and not to come to an agreement.

Trade union delegates (*délégués syndicaux*)

Trade union delegates may be appointed only in companies of fifty or more employees, unless otherwise stipulated by collective agreement. Trade union delegates are appointed by the relevant trade union and not by the section within the company. The number of delegates appointed varies from one to five, according to the size of the work force. There is no fixed mandate, and delegates must be over 18 years of age, have one year's seniority within the company and not be related to the employer.

Duties of trade union delegates. By law, trade union delegates must represent their union to the employer, but in practice they can intervene on all matters relating to the material and moral well-being of the employees, whether unionized or not. They have consultation rights on such matters as the reorganization of working time and changes in working conditions. They also have negotiating rights in that they will form part of the employee delegation when negotiating with the employer on pay, matters relating to pay and working time and conditions.

Rights of trade union delegates. Trade union delegates are entitled to time off in order to carry out union activities ranging from ten to twenty hours a month, according to the size of the company. They also enjoy protection against dismissal during their term of office and for twelve months following the end of their mandate. Candidates for the appointment of trade union delegate are protected against dismissal for six months following their candidature.

Employers' organizations

The main national employers' organization is the CNPF (*Conseil Nationale du Patronat Français*), which represents around 75 per cent of French employers. The CNPF does not bargain directly, except on national framework agreements, but does issue an annual statement on pay: since 1986 this has not included a recommended percentage. Two employer organizations represent small and middle-size companies: the CGPME (*Confédération Générale des Petites et Moyennes Entreprises*) and the SNPMI (*Syndicat National du Patronat Moderne et Indépendant*).

Employer associations at sectoral level are involved in the negotiation of minimum pay and conditions, and may issue pay recommendations for company-level bargaining. Two of the most prominent industrial associations are, in chemicals, the *Union des Industries Chimiques* (UIC) and in metalworking the *Union des Industries Métallurgiques et Minières* (UIMM).

Collective bargaining

Main levels of bargaining

Bargaining is conducted at three levels: national, industry and company. At *national* level, tripartite multi-industry agreements are concluded between central employers and trade union organizations. These agreements are not binding but set frameworks within which sectoral and company bargaining can take place: subjects covered include working time flexibility, sex equality and training. At *sectoral* level there is an annual obligation, under the 1982 Auroux laws, to negotiate on minimum rates of pay, other elements of pay and working time. However, there is no obligation to conclude an agreement and employers will sometimes unilaterally impose minimum rate increases. Some sectoral employers' organizations, such as in metalworking, make annual pay recommendations which usually do not give a figure but serve to guide companies in their pay bargaining. (Pay bargaining is dealt with in greater depth in the fourth volume of the European Management Guides series.)

The 1982 legislation also includes an obligation for the parties at industry level to review job classification systems every five years, but, again, not necessarily to agree to any changes. Indeed, many industries have job classification systems dating from the 1950s. The government recently called upon industries to update their classification systems. The results have been positive in many industries, such as metalworking, which overhauled its classification system in 1990 in order to facilitate career progression.

At *company* level the 1982 legislation lays an annual obligation on employers to bargain annually with union representatives, if they exist within the company, or workers' representatives, on pay. As at sectoral level, however, there is no obligation to conclude an agreement. If desired, agreements can also be negotiated on issues such as bonus schemes, working time, job classifications, trade union rights, terms and conditions of employment, the right of expression, workers' representation and training. According to a Ministry of Labour survey, company bargaining has been on the increase in recent years, with 3,937 agreements signed in 1990, compared with 3,499 in 1989.

Collective agreements

Under the Labour Code, collective agreements are agreements relating to conditions of work and social guarantees concluded between employers and representative trade unions, at national, regional, local or plant level. There are two types: a *convention collective* deals with all terms and conditions whereas an *accord collectif* deals with a single issue, such as pay or working time. Collective agreements are most common at industry level and usually improve upon the statutory position on matters such as holiday provision, time-off rights, and severance payments. These agreements in turn set a floor for company practice. Sectoral collective agreements are binding once signed by one or more recognized representative unions and an employers' organization or individual employer. Therefore an agreement can be validated by the signature of one minority union. However, unions do have a right to veto company agreements under the 1982 Auroux laws as long as the union obtained at least 50 per cent of the eligible number of votes (not the number of votes actually cast) in the most recent elections to the company's works committee, and provided that it does so within one week of the agreement being signed.

Collective agreements can be extended by ministerial decree to all companies, whether they have signed or not, within the same sector and geographical area (*procedure d'extension*) or to all companies in the same sector but in a different geographical area (*procedure d'élargissement*). The latter will usually take place in cases where attempts to sign an agreement in that area have failed. These procedures are designed to give the Ministry of Labour a certain amount of control over the content of collective agreements, as certain conditions must be met before they can be extended, such as the inclusion of anti-discrimination and equal pay rights.

Collective agreements usually cover a twelve-month period and are automatically renewed unless notice to terminate is given. Some agreements, such as the engineering agreements for blue-collar workers in Paris, forbid strikes and lock-outs during the period of notice preceding the termination of the agreement. However, 'peace clauses' forbidding industrial action during the lifetime of an agreement are uncommon.

Industrial action

All private-sector employees and most public-sector employees, except those in the police force, and prison and security services, have a constitutionally guaranteed right to strike. Apart from this provision, industrial action is not generally subject to statutory regulation, and case law plays a major role in determining whether action is lawful.

Lawful and unlawful action

A strike is defined as entailing a total stoppage of work. Strikes are lawful only if conducted in pursuit of industrial demands (*fondée sur des revendications professionnelles*). Employees are required to present their demands to the employer before taking action but they are not obliged to wait for a reaction or give notice, except in the public services (see below).

Strikes undertaken for political reasons are not legal unless directed against the government's social and economic policy (court rulings of 29 July 1979 and 12 January 1971); most sympathy strikes (*grèves de solidarité*) are also illegal unless they are in support of demands deemed to be of direct relevance to the striking employees, either through being members of the same organization or in pursuit of broader objectives. Sympathy action over a sectoral collective agreement would generally be legal. Rotating strikes (*grèves tournantes*) are forbidden in the public sector but have been recognized by the courts as generally legal in the private sector (rulings of 11 October 1957 and 16 July 1964) unless the motive for the strike is deemed to be to disrupt production seriously or to endanger the safety of the company. Go-slows or 'irritation strikes' (*grèves perlées*) are not considered as strikes under the definition of a total stoppage of work and the courts have viewed them as a failure to perform the employee's obligations (rulings of 7 March 1984, 3 July 1984 and 8 October 1987). Unannounced and repeated short stoppages (*débrayages inopinés et répétés*) are deemed legal as long as the motive of the action is not to harm or disrupt the company (ruling of 25 February 1988). Sit-ins (*grèves avec occupation des locaux de travail*) are generally deemed by case law to be illegal unless the action does not hinder the running of the company. Wildcat strikes (*grèves sauvages*) are deemed legal in that they are total stoppages of work and there is no legal obligation for employees to give notice of strike action or go through formal union procedures: employees in the private sector do not have to give any notice before taking industrial action, nor are they obliged by law to wait for the outcome of conciliation or organize a ballot.

Public-sector employees must give five days' notice before industrial action is taken. In certain industries, such as television broadcasting and air traffic control, a skeleton service must be maintained. Some collective agreements in the private sector, however, also contain restrictive clauses requiring notice of a strike to be given: for example, the agreement covering road haulage requires one week's notice and the agreement covering chemicals stipulates that ten clear days must elapse between the beginning of conciliation and a strike.

By law (Labour Code, article 512–1) the act of going on strike does not constitute a breach of contract, and under the law of 25 July 1985 employees have the right to be reinstated if found to have been unfairly dismissed for striking. Employers are under no obligation to pay employees for the period during which they are out on strike. However, they must carry on paying those not on strike even if their work is disrupted by strikers (cases of 14 March 1971 and 25 January 1978). Employers may be relieved of this obligation if it is deemed impossible to offer work to employees, for example if machines are not running or if the employer has applied for an injunction to remove pickets or workers engaged in sit-ins. French unions do not generally grant strike pay and so disputes tend to consist of short stoppages, meaning that France loses comparatively few working days to industrial conflicts (in 1987 twenty-nine per 1,000 employees, compared with 163 per 1,000 in the UK).

Lock-outs

Lock-outs are generally held by case law to be illegal, and an employer might be liable to pay employees for any period during which they were locked out. However, lock-outs have been ruled to be legal under certain circumstances, such as where a strike by employees caused a total breakdown in the functioning of the company (case of 25 February 1988) or threatened the safety of staff or other persons and property (case of 7 November 1990).

Consequences of industrial action

Employees cannot be dismissed for legal industrial action (see above), nor does it constitute a breach of contract. Rather, the contracts of striking employees are deemed to be suspended.

Employees who have damaged stock, assaulted supervisors or threatened other employees during the course of a strike are liable to summary dismissal for flagrant misconduct (*faute lourde*). Strikers participating in illegal strikes may also be liable to summary dismissal for flagrant misconduct.

If the majority of the work force vote to return to work, a minority may continue to strike as long as they make new demands of the employer, assuming that the employer has met the original demands.

Conciliation machinery

Three complementary procedures for the settling of disputes are provided for by law: conciliation, mediation and arbitration. Many collective agreements set out *conciliation* procedures which must be adhered to before strike action can be taken. If no such provision exists, parties to a dispute may go before a regional or national conciliation committee (*commission regionale/nationale de conciliation* – under the labour Code, article L 523–3). This procedure is voluntary but, if conciliation procedures are engaged, both parties are obliged to appear in person. Conciliation will lead to either agreement or failure, in which case the matter can be taken either to mediation or straight to arbitration.

A matter may be taken to *mediation* by the parties at their own initiative or by the Minister of Labour or *préfet* at the written request of the parties. The mediator is chosen by the minister (at national level, in the case, for example, of collective agreements) or the *préfet* (at regional or local level). The mediator will bring the parties together and then has one month in which to issue a recommendation. This recommendation is not binding and the parties are entitled to reject it within eight days, giving their reasons for doing so. If this is the case, the results are communicated by the mediator to the relevant authorities within forty-eight hours and made public within three months.

Arbitration mechanisms may be provided for in a collective agreement but, if not, a matter which has not been resolved at either conciliation or mediation level may be taken to arbitration if both parties wish. The arbitrator is chosen by the parties and will reach a decision, stating the reasons behind it. This decision is binding, and can be contested by the parties, in the eight days following the decision, in the high arbitration court (*cour supérieure d'arbitrage*) only if the ruling breaches the law or goes beyond the arbitrator's remit.

Collective dismissal

Dismissal of under ten employees over a period of thirty days

If an employer intends to make between two and nine employees redundant over a period of thirty days, staff representatives or the works committee, if one exists, must be consulted in a meeting before the employees concerned are notified. The employer must give information concerning the reasons for dismissal, measures taken to avoid it, such as early retirement or retraining contracts, the criteria used in selecting employees for redundancy, the number to be dismissed, the order of dismissals and the expected date. Representatives must be informed of the meeting three days beforehand. After the meeting, employee representatives may draw up a report on the proposed employer action and can make use of experts, such as accountants. The report is then forwarded to the departmental labour authority (*directeur départemental du travail*).

Employers must send employees they propose to make redundant a registered letter requesting attendance at an interview, specifying the purpose, date, time and place of interview. At the interview the employer must explain the reasons for dismissal and offer a retraining contract to enhance their skills and facilitate future job placement; the scheme is jointly funded by the state, unemployment insurance organizations and companies. The employee has between fifteen and twenty-one days, depending on the overall numbers being made redundant, to respond to this offer. The employer must give employees written notice of redundancy no sooner than seven full days after the interview (fifteen days in the case of a manager). The employer must then inform the labour inspectorate of the redundancy within eight days of the redundancy letters being sent out.

Dismissal of at least ten employees over a period of thirty days

If an employer wishes to dismiss ten or more employees over a period of thirty days, two consultative meetings must be held with staff representatives or works committees. The meetings must be separated by no more than:

- Fourteen days if the redundancies are fewer than 100.
- Twenty-one days if the redundancies total 100–249.
- Twenty-eight days if the redundancies total 250 or more.

Before the first meeting the employer must provide representatives with all relevant information concerning the redundancies and their justification. The employer must also outline the terms of a social compensation plan, which must by law be drawn up to limit redundancies: this will cover measures such as short-time working, voluntary redundancy and retraining. At the first meeting the employer is obliged to study suggestions made by the works committee to limit redundancies. At the second meeting the employer must give exact details concerning those to be made redundant and the date and order of dismissal. The representative will then draw up a report, drawing, if required, upon the services of an accountant (*expert-comptable*), which is given to the departmental labour authorities and will be referred to in the case of a dispute. Individual letters notifying redundancy must not be sent out until the staff representatives have been consulted. In the absence of a staff representative or works committee, details of redundancies must be passed on to the departmental labour authorities along with the official notification of redundancy.

　The employer must send all necessary information to the labour inspectorate at least one day after the first meeting with staff representatives or the works committee, such as details and minutes of the consultation meeting. After the second consultation meeting, employers must send the labour inspectorate all details of the proposed redundancies and measures taken to reduce the impact of the redundancies.

　The employer may not formally notify employees of redundancy until thirty to sixty days, depending on the scale of the redundancies, after the labour inspectorate has examined the information sent by the employer. However, the inspectorate's role is essentially to ensure that the procedures are followed correctly, and that appropriate attention has been paid to the needs of employees affected: its authorization is not required for the dismissals as such.

Severance pay

Employees are entitled to severance pay (*indemnité de licenciement*) provided they have at least two years' continuous service, have not been summarily dismissed and have been employed on a permanent contract. Minimum severance payments are determined by law as one tenth of a month's salary per year of service for monthly paid employees, or twenty hours' salary per year of service for hourly paid workers. Employees in the private sector are also entitled to an additional payment of one fifteenth of a month's salary for each additional year of service over ten. However, many collective agreements provide for higher severance payments, typically one fifth of a month's salary per year of service, increasing to a quarter after five years' service. All severance payments are lump sums and exempt from tax or social security contributions.

Transfer of undertakings

In law (Labour Code, article 432–1), employers must consult the works committee before any decision is taken involving 'a change in the economic or legal organization of the company', such as a merger, an acquisition, selling off or acquiring a subsidiary, or any other significant change relating to the structure of a company's production. All contracts in force on the day of the transfer remain in force on the same terms and conditions. However, the new employer is entitled to make employees redundant, and this may be linked with any rationalization of the firm following the transfer (for example, as the consequence of a merger). Employers can also propose a variation in the terms of an individual's contract which might lead to termination if the employee refused to accept the changes.

Appendix

Ministry of Labour:
127 rue de Grenelle
75700 Paris
tel. + 33 1 40 56 60 00

Agence Nationale pour l'Emploi
(ANPE):
23 rue Félix
Paris 75009
tel. + 33 1 49 31 74 00

CGT–Force Ouvrière:
198 avenue du Maine
75014 Paris Cédex 14
tel. + 33 1 45 39 22 03

CFDT:
4 boulevard de la Villette,
75955 Paris Cédex 19
tel. + 33 1 42 03 80 00

CGT:
263 rue de Paris
93516 Montreuil Cédex
tel. +33 1 48 51 80 00

Confédération Générale
des Cadres:
30 rue de Gramont
75002 Paris
tel. + 33 1 42 61 81 76

Conseil National du Patronat
Français (national employers'
organization):
31 rue Pierre 1er de Serbie
Paris 75016
tel. + 33 1 40 69 44 44

British Chamber of Commerce:
8 rue Cimerosa
75118 Paris
tel. + 33 1 45 05 13 08
fax + 33 1 45 53 02 87

4
Germany

German industrial relations, including both participation mechanisms and collective bargaining, are characterized by a high degree of statutory regulation, complemented and developed by a large body of case law which is decisive on some major issues, such as the lawfulness of industrial action. Employee interests are represented through a dual system of statutory works councils at workplace level and free collective bargaining, mostly on an industry basis, via trade unions. Both paths are highly interrelated in practice. This is complemented by a structure of board-level representation which has less impact on day-to-day industrial relations.

Both employer and trade union organizations are strong, representative and disciplined. Despite conflicts over major strategic issues, such as shorter hours in the mid-1980s, the day-to-day conduct of industrial relations, especially at workplace level, remains highly consensual. And although employees have extensive statutory rights at the workplace, German managers are held to exercise greater control over production processes, for example, than their UK counterparts have traditionally been able to do. However – and contrary to popular stereotypes – German management styles have also been found to be more collegial, informal and participatory than those in the UK and France. Both facets are a function of institutional factors, such as an absence of craft unionism and the need to recognize and live with statutory employee rights. Both managerial control and pragmatic informality are also fostered by broader features of the industrial culture, in which a skilled work force is willing to recognize corporate objectives in return for institutionalized rights and participation in the technological rent earned by the German economy in the international division of labour. (See too 'Selected further reading' at the end of this volume.)

In the past, German trade unionists often looked to the UK as providing an example of independent unions, well implanted at workplace level through strong shop stewards' organizations and not hamstrung by 'corporatist' institutions, such as works councils, which were seen as divisive mechanisms for undermining union influence. However, although eroded by structural changes in industry, trade unionism in Germany has proved to be among the most resilient in Europe since 1980, and established union and social rights – although weakened and qualified in some areas – have remained largely intact.

In the mid-1980s the structure of industrial relations and bargaining was widely criticized both within, and even more outside, Germany as part of a pattern of institutional rigidities which were responsible for slow growth and a draining away of economic dynamism. The ability of industry to take advantage of the investment boom triggered by the single market programme appeared to have confounded these critics. However, the wholesale implanting of the West German industrial relations system in the former German Democratic Republic will prove a stern test of its durability and flexibility in both East and West in the coming decade.

National-level co-operation and consultation

There is no formal national tripartite or bipartite forum for consultation or negotiation on pay or industrial relations involving the government, the central employers' organization, the BDA, or the principal trade union centre, the DGB. 'Concerted Action', a tripartite process to assess economic developments and shape pay bargaining as part of the economic Stability Law introduced under the 1966–69 Grand Coalition of Social Democrats, Liberals and the two Conservative parties, was abandoned by the trade unions in 1977, ostensibly because of employer attempts to have industrial participation declared unconstitutional. A role in the end of Concerted Action was also played, however, by the growing strains on union cohesiveness of implied pay norms – highlighted by the oil crisis and a series of wildcat strikes in the period 1969–73. Nevertheless, a form of Concerted Action – by name – has continued as a forum for discussion in the health service.

Although there is no formal structure of tripartism, the heavily legally regulated character of German industrial relations produces a focus on the state, and implies consultation and discussion on

legislation – although by no means consensus. The scale of
economic difficulties confronting East Germany, and the need
to produce solutions able to command broad support, have
encouraged contacts between the Conservative–Liberal coalition
government and trade unions which had cooled markedly in the
mid-1980s. Whether this could form the core of a new tripartite
accord will depend on developments in the East, and the extent
to which the costs of unity impose financial constraints – higher
taxes, pressure for wage restraint – in the West. As we discuss in
the section on bargaining in this book and in the fourth book in
the series, on pay determination, there are strong institutional and
economic forces which push towards effective, if informal, forms of
national co-ordination on pay issues.

Industrial participation

Employee participation, which covers a variety of degrees of
involvement ranging from information to 'co-determination', takes
place via two institutions: through separate employee-only works
councils (*Betriebsräte*) at workplace, company or group level, and
through employee representation on the supervisory boards of
companies. Of the two, the most directly and practically relevant
– both for managements and for employees – is the works council
system.

There is no formal involvement by trade unions in the day-to-day
operation of the works councils' structure, though the informal
and practical links are an essential element in the operation
both of statutory participation and of collective bargaining: these
aspects are looked at below. However, trade unions have statutory
rights of access to company premises, and may attend works
meetings. Employers and works councils must co-operate both with
unions and with employers' organizations. A trade union is also
entitled to take an employer to court and obtain a court order under
the Works Constitution Act, 1972, should the employer grossly
violate their obligations under the act. Trade unions do, however,
have representation rights at supervisory board level under the
Codetermination Act, 1976, which applies to large public
companies (see pages 78–80 below).

Workplace employee representation

Works councils

Works councils represent one of the most characteristic features of German industrial relations and constitute one arm of the 'dual' structure. Originally a product of the factory council movement during the 1918 revolution, they became a core element of the institutional structure of the Weimar Republic (1919–33). They were revived and given a new statutory basis in 1952 by the Adenauer government, although opposed in that form by the Social Democrats and Communist Party on the grounds that the new system conferred insufficient rights and was aimed at weakening trade unionism at plant level. Works councils' rights were considerably enhanced by the Social Democrat government under Willy Brandt in 1972, and it is that year's Works Constitution Act (*Betriebsverfassungsgesetz*), subsequently amended by the Conservative–Liberal coalition in the 1980s, which governs the current structure and powers of works councils.

Works councils are employee-only bodies, directly elected by the work force, for an individual establishment (*Betrieb*): this may be coterminous with a company, but could cover an individual plant within a multi-plant firm, one department store within a chain, or a distinct works on a single site characterized by several types of operation. Where a company consists of several establishments, each with its own works council, a works council for the company as a whole (central works council, *Gesamtbetriebsrat*) can be formed by delegation from individual works councils. Similarly, if the company is part of a group, a group – or combine – works council (*Konzernbetriebsrat*) can be set up by delegation.

Works councils are not mandatory. Rather, they may be elected in any establishment with at least five eligible employees. Once elected, however, they must be recognized by the employer. The law requires that the employer and the works council should meet at least monthly, and puts both sides under an obligation to seek to resolve differences in good faith.

The costs of operating works councils are borne by the employer. This embraces the provision of office space and facilities, office personnel and meeting other costs incurred by the works council. Examples include:

- Appropriate travel costs.
- Consultation with a lawyer or other expert.
- Printing costs for works council literature (although not a regular publication).
- Any necessary specialist literature, including that published by trade unions in the area of employment law or industrial relations.
- Costs of hiring an interpreter for works meetings if needed.

Where the establishment employs from five to twenty employees only one representative may be elected. The size of the works council then increases with establishment size, ranging from five members in establishments with fifty-one to one hundred and fifty employees to fifteen members where there are 1,001–2,000 employees, and thirty-one members for work forces between 7,001 and 9,000. Where the establishment employs more than 9,000 employees an additional two members can be added for each additional 3,000 employees.

Establishments which are concerned mainly with charitable, political, scientific or cultural activities, or which serve to express opinions or are engaged in journalistic reportage, are not covered by the 1972 law if the character of the establishment makes it inappropriate: in German these are collectively referred to as *Tendenzbetriebe*. The public sector is covered by separate legislation for employee representation.

Eligible employees are all blue and white-collar workers employed by the establishment, together with trainees. The definition excludes members of a firm's management board, owners, or individuals employed at the workplace for other than principally economic reasons. The provisions of the Works Constitution Act do not apply to 'executives' (*leitende Angestellte*), who since 1989 have been able to elect their own representative institution (see below). Executives are also a separate category for the purposes of board-level representation under the Codetermination Act, 1976 (see below). Under a recent amendment to the Works Constitution Act an executive is any employee who:

- May hire or dismiss on their own authority.
- Has a general authority to conduct business on behalf of the undertaking.
- Carries out tasks deemed to be significant for the existence or development of the undertaking, calling for particular experience or knowledge.
- Exercises decisions largely free of direct instruction.

In the event of doubt, an executive is anyone:

- Employed at a level of management in which other employees are classified as 'executives'.
- In receipt of a salary which is the norm for executives in that enterprise, or
- In receipt of a salary which is at least three times the social security calculation base (DM 120,960, or £41,000 in 1991).

In some industries the trade unions, managers' organizations and employers' associations have agreed a set of specific criteria to implement the law.

Works councils consist of blue-collar workers (*Arbeiter*) and white-collar workers (*Angestellte*) in proportion to their numbers in the establishment, with certain minimum requirements. Election is direct and by secret ballot, with the work force voting for representatives in their category. Where both groups agree, this group voting can be relaxed, with the whole work force in one election. In practice, as we also discuss below, DGB-affiliated trade unions supply the bulk of the candidates for works councils, usually in the form of approved slates, and also a majority, around 65 per cent, of elected representatives. Non-DGB unions account for a further 6–7 per cent of representatives. According to the 1972 Act, the composition of the works council should reflect both the different occupations active in the establishment and the proportion of male to female workers. However, this is not a mandatory quota, and in practice women are underrepresented as works councillors. Separate elections take place for youth representatives.

The coverage of the work force by works council representation is limited by a number of factors. Firstly, an estimated quarter of the working population is employed in establishments which are either too small to meet the size threshold, are excluded because of the nature of their activities (the *Tendenzbetriebe*), or are in the public sector. Secondly, the fact that works councils are not mandatory leaves scope for employees to exercise their free will (and for employers to create a climate which is either hostile or which seeks to make statutory representation superfluous). Estimates of coverage vary: according to a 1980 survey, around 66 per cent of private-sector employees worked in an establishment with a works council. The incidence of works councils varies markedly by size and location, with many smaller establishments outside larger towns and cities operating without a works council.

Executive representation committees

In 1984 the Federal Constitutional Court found that the system of candidacy in elections to works councils, which required a minimum number of signatures, did not grant equality of access to all individuals and organizations. As a consequence the Christian Democrat–Liberal coalition negotiated an amendment to the 1972 Act intended to rectify the problem. The eventual 1988 amendment in fact contained a package of changes, and was widely seen by commentators as representing a *quid pro quo* within the coalition in which the Liberals (FDP) made concessions to the so-called 'social wing' of the Christian Democrats on legislation to keep certain companies under the more rigorous board-level employee participation regime applicable in the coal, iron and steel industries (see below) in return for greater rights for 'minorities' in works council elections, and specifically for separate representation for executives (already defined above). Managers' organizations, in particular the Union der Leitenden Angestellten (ULA), had long been pressing for the change.

The 1988 amendment allowed executives, who on the definition set out above account on average for 2–3 per cent of the work force, to establish executive representation committees (*Sprecherausschüsse*, shortened below to ERCs) in any establishment with at least ten executives. There are provisions for setting up ERCs at company or group level. The first elections under the new provision took place in spring 1990. In all, 568 ERCs were elected, in many cases merely ratifying long-standing voluntary arrangements.

ERCs have the following rights:

- A right to information needed by the committee to exercise their statutory tasks, given 'comprehensively and in good time' and backed up by relevant documentation.
- Individual executives have a right to inspect their personal files, accompanied if requested by an ERC member, and append their own observations.
- ERCs and employers can agree upon written guidelines for the commencement and termination of managers' contracts which are then binding on the company. The ERC must also be informed of any appointments or changes in the employment of executives.
- The employer must inform the ERC of changes in systems of remuneration, employee appraisal, or other general conditions of employment.
- The employer must notify all terminations of employment to the ERC, which has a week to respond: any termination not notified is null and void.
- The employer must inform the ERC of the economic circumstances of the company at least once a year, and of any changes which might be prejudicial to the interests of executives, together with proposals for mitigating the disadvantages.

Status of work-force representatives

Works councillors are elected for a period of four years. Above 300 employees, and depending on the size of the establishment, the employer must release a certain number of councillors on pay for works council activities either full or part-time: such activities must not be confined to the plant – for example, they would include court proceedings, or consultations with the authorities or with trade unions, but not for collective bargaining or to attend purely trade union functions. The number of employees released for works council activities ranges from one (300–600 employees) to three (1,001–2,000 employees), and up to eleven in establishments with 9,000–10,000 employees, with an extra member released for each 2,000 employees above that limit. The numbers may be increased or the thresholds changed by collective – that is, usually, industry – agreement or by local 'works' agreement.

Works council members also have a right to:

- Continuing access to training, with scope to catch up with training missed while released from work for works council duties.
- Relevant training and education to carry out their duties. These are often provided by the trade unions, but companies also provide training (for example, in job evaluation, as grading is subject to co-determination). If the employer objects to the choice of course, they can obtain a binding ruling from a conciliation committee (see below). All works council members also have an automatic right to three weeks off during their period of office to attend courses approved by the local labour authorities in conjunction with trade unions and employers' associations.

Works councillors are protected by law against dismissal. Under the Protection against Dismissal Act, 1969, members of works councils and youth representatives are protected from ordinary dismissal during their period of office and for a year after. Any employer's application for summary dismissal of a works councillor requires works council approval: the employer may go to the courts to overrule a works council objection. Candidates, too, are protected against ordinary dismissal from the date of nomination until six months after the election results are published.

Works councils' role

Duties of the works council. One major difference between statutory employee representation through works councils and bargaining or representation by trade unions is the obligation on works councils to co-operate with the employer 'for the good of the employees and the establishment' and for both employer and works council to refrain from acts of 'industrial warfare . . . or activities that imperil the tranquillity of the establishment'. However, although they are formally subject to this absolute peace obligation, and cannot call a strike, and in practice and for the most part function on a co-operative basis with employers, works councils do possess informal sanctions based on their statutory powers. The mere possibility of such negative powers being evoked, matched by employers' ability to grant or withhold a variety of concessions, creates the basis for an informal resolution of conflicts in which full-time works council members, especially the chair, play a major role.

Works councils are statutorily enjoined:

- To ensure compliance with laws, collective agreements and works agreements for the benefit of employees.
- To make recommendations to the employer on actions to benefit employees and the establishment.
- To promote the rehabilitation and integration of people with disabilities, older workers, and foreign workers.

The works council must also call a meeting of employees, either in the whole establishment or at department level, at least once a quarter, to which the employer is invited. The employer has to be given a copy of the agenda, and is also entitled to address the meetings. At least once a year the employer must present a report to a work force meeting, covering staff questions and social matters in the establishment (see below), together with a presentation on the business situation of the firm. The works council must notify any trade union represented in the plant of proposed works meetings, and union officials are entitled to attend in an advisory capacity.

Confidentiality. Both during and after their period of office, works council members may not disclose outside the works council, or make use of, any genuine trade or business secrets which are expressly identified as such by the employer. These could, for example, include information on pay and labour costs. How the case of a proposed closure or merger might be treated would depend on case law and the specific circumstances involved. Confidentiality also applies to any information gained about individual employees as a result of the exercise of co-determination or obtained direct from an employee seeking advice or help from the works council.

Rights and powers of the works council. Works councils have a panoply of rights, ranging from information through participation in decisions to joint decision-making ('co-determination' – in German, *Mitbestimmung*), depending, formally, on the size of establishment and the issue. Below we examine the main rights by subject area, with the emphasis on the strongest rights, and indicate the thresholds beyond which certain rights are applicable. The principal rights are:

- *The right to be heard (Anhörungsrecht)*. Works councils have rights to express opinions on issues as well as initiate proposals in some areas.
- *Information.* Works councils have a general right to be informed 'comprehensively and in good time' on any matters necessary for them to carry out their duties. Information must precede any employer decision and cannot be a mere formality.
- *Consultation (Beratungsrecht).* The final decision remains with the employer, but employers must seek the works council's views, identify issues for possible negotiation, and balance their interests with those of the work force.
- *Co-determination (Mitbestimmung)* takes place through the exercise of various types of right, including the works council's right to object to an employer proposal: in essence, it means that the employer may not proceed with an action without the assent of the works council or a decision from a Labour Court or conciliation committee in its stead.

Conciliation committees (*Einigungsstelle*) – something of a misnomer in that they can issue binding rulings – may be established as and when required, or on a permanent basis, and typically consist of equal numbers of employer/employee representatives, chaired by an independent figure – usually a local Labour Court Judge. In general, recourse to this machinery is rare, and the parties prefer to keep negotiating, with at least the prospect of shaping the outcome. (According to one study from the mid-1970s, conciliation committees were never set up or called on in 82 per cent of all undertakings, and in the remainder only infrequently.) Conciliation committees cannot decide on matters of law.

In some instances both parties are required, or may choose, to come to a formal written agreement termed a 'works agreement' (*Betriebsvereinbarung*). Under the Works Constitution Act, 'works agreements shall not deal with remuneration and other conditions of employment that have been fixed or are normally fixed by collective agreement' (*Tarifvertrag*) unless a collective agreement expressly authorizes it. Works agreements therefore represent a tier of collective provision which is, in theory, one rung below that of collective agreements negotiated between trade unions and employers or employers' associations. Nevertheless, works agreements are mandatory and directly applicable, and entitlements granted under them cannot be forfeited: unlike collective agreements, they can be tested in the courts on grounds of equity. Also, unlike collective agreements, they can be terminated at any time upon three months' notice.

As well as regulating the matters identified below, works agreements can also cover such issues as pensions, financial participation by employees, the introduction of team working, environmental matters, social benefits and equal treatment programmes.

Co-determination on social matters. The strongest set of rights – co-determination – apply in the area of 'social matters'. Co-determination here means that the employer and works council *must* come to an agreement on the following issues, unless they are already exhaustively regulated by law or collective agreement. Where no agreement is possible the matter is settled by a binding ruling of a conciliation committee. That is, no unilateral management decision is valid in these areas. There is extensive case law both supporting and clarifying the application of these rights. The main social matters are:

- The start and finish of daily working time, breaks and shift patterns, holiday arrangements.
- Temporary increases or decreases in normal working hours (i.e. overtime and short time).
- The timing and form of the payment of remuneration.
- The 'introduction and use of technical devices designed to monitor the behaviour and performance of employees'.
- Health and safety arrangements.
- The 'form, structure and administration' of company social benefits.
- 'Remuneration arrangements', including the 'principles of remuneration' and the 'introduction and application of new remuneration systems'.
- The fixing of rates under payment-by-results systems.

Co-determination, information, consultation on job design and the work environment. Works councils must be informed of and consulted on plans concerning changes to premises, plant, work processes or jobs. Under a 1988 amendment, consultation must include scope for due consideration to be given to works council suggestions and reservations. The works council has a right of co-determination over measures to mitigate, obviate or compensate for any burden imposed on employees as a result of changes to jobs, work processes or the work environment which 'are in obvious contradiction to the established findings of ergonomics'.

Information, consultation and co-determination on personnel matters. Works councils can exercise considerable influence over personnel management and directly impinge on areas customarily viewed as the prerogative of the employer in the United Kingdom. In many respects the influence of works councils is at its most profound in this field. Firstly, the rights acquired can give works councils considerable leverage in this and other areas of workplace relations. And secondly, not only can works councils shape internal labour markets but also, by institutionalizing the power of 'insiders', they can also affect the broader labour market. Rights, set out more specifically below, can be exercised in the areas of: personnel planning, vacancies and recruitment, the engagement of staff, transfers and regrading, and individual dismissals.

Personnel planning. There is a right to information and to make recommendations on personnel planning, including forecast personnel needs, any staff changes or movements, and vocational training, together with a right of consultation to avoid employee hardship. Proposals must be backed up by 'relevant documentation'.

Recruitment. Works councils can ask for all vacancies to be first advertised internally before external recruitment begins, although both sides may formally agree to exclude certain categories of employee from this provision. Failure to advertise internally may give the works council grounds for withholding consent to an appointment (see below). Any application forms, or staff questionnaires, require the approval of the works council: the employer must obtain a ruling from a conciliation committee if consent is not granted. Guidelines for selection (together with transfer, regrading or dismissal) drawn up by an employer require works council approval. In establishments with fewer than 1,000 employees the employer is free to decide whether or not to set out formal guidelines: however, in larger organizations the works council has a right to request such guidelines, with the option of a conciliation ruling if the parties cannot agree.

Engagement, transfer, regrading. In establishments with more than twenty employees the works council must be informed of any proposed engagement or movement of staff, and in the case of engagement must be shown any application and selection documents. The works council may refuse to approve the proposal on a number of grounds, such as breach of existing guidelines, disadvantage to existing employees, failure to advertise internally, and fears that the individual might be disruptive to social and industrial peace in the establishment. The works council has a week in which to respond, and the employer must obtain a decision from a labour court to overrule a withholding of consent. (There are procedures which allow an appointment to be made without works council consent in an emergency, but the employer must subsequently justify it.) Works councils' co-determination rights in this area do not apply to executives (as defined above): however, the works council must still be informed of such appointments or staff changes.

The works council also has a right of co-determination over what individual information may be contained in written contracts of employment.

Recruitment issues are dealt with in detail in the first volume in the European Management Guides series.

Individual dismissal. All dismissals must be notified, with the reasons for dismissal, to the works council. Any dismissal which is not notified is null and void. The works council has a week to respond in writing to an 'ordinary dismissal' (that is, with notice) and three days to respond to a summary dismissal. The works council can oppose the planned dismissal for a number of reasons, including:

- Inadequate consideration of the social aspects in the selection of an employee for dismissal.
- Breach of an agreed guideline.
- The possibility of continued employment either elsewhere in the establishment or company and/or after a reasonable amount of training.
- If the employee, where agreeable, could be retained with changed terms of employment.

Works council opposition to a dismissal cannot stop the action as such. However, should the employee seek to contest the dismissal through the courts with the support of the works council, the employer must offer the employee work at unchanged terms until final settlement of the case. (For exemptions and details, see the European Management Guide *Terms and Conditions of Employment*, pp. 94–5.)

Information rights on financial and business matters. In all *companies*, not establishments, with more than 100 permanent employees a sub-committee of the works council known as the Economic Committee (*Wirtschaftsausschuss*) may be established to deal specifically with information from the employer on the state of the business. Employers are required to give information on the financial state of the business 'in full and in good time', supported by appropriate documentation, as long as it does not compromise business secrecy, and spell out the implications for personnel planning. Issues on which information must be given include:

- The economic and financial situation of the company.
- The product and marketing situation.
- Investment, production and rationalization plans, including new work methods.
- Reductions in activities, closures, or transfers of operations.

The works council can obtain a ruling from a conciliation committee should an employer refuse to divulge information. After consultation with the economic committee, employers must also inform employees directly on the state of the business: in companies with more than 1,000 employees this has to happen in writing at least once a quarter; in firms with more than twenty employees, information can be presented orally. Failure to provide information which is legally required, or to present it incomplete or delayed, can make the employer liable to a fine of up to DM 20,000 (£6,780).

Consultation and co-determination in the event of redundancies. In companies with twenty or more employees the employer must inform the works council of, and consult on, any changes to the business – principally reductions in operations, closures, transfers and amalgamations, together with new work processes – which may entail 'substantial disadvantages' for the work force, or a large proportion of it.

The employer and works council must seek to reconcile their interests, and may formally agree on the general principles to be applied in making the proposed changes. The works council also has an enforceable right of co-determination in the negotiation of a 'social compensation plan' (*Sozialplan*) to compensate employees for any financial losses. This area is dealt with in detail below in the section on 'Collective dismissal'.

Works councils and the trade unions. German trade unions are not formally or legally anchored in the workplace as organizations, and trade union plant representatives (*Vertrauensleute*) have no recognized role in bargaining or representation comparable with that of British shop stewards. Rather, they act as a local base for their respective trade union, and serve as a two-way transmission mechanism between the union and its members on issues such as pay claims: since works councils are forbidden to initiate industrial action, shop stewards often take responsibility for co-ordinating official strikes at plant level, as well as occasionally being a catalyst of more 'spontaneous' – but technically unlawful – action. In practice, shop stewards work closely with works councils, reflecting the fact that most works councillors are union members. In large plants shop stewards may establish a formal shop stewards' committee with a convenor (*Vertrauenskörperleitung*).

Around seventy collective agreements and works agreements make provision for either dismissal protection or facilities for shop stewards, with the main areas covered in engineering, printing, the clothing industry and the postal service.

The 'new industrial relations'

Initiatives to see what benefits could be derived from the application of the 'new industrial relations' to German industry have been widespread in the 1980s. In 1986 the chemical employers' association Bundesverband Chemie issued a discussion document on team working, and Gesamtmetall, the central employers' organization in metalworking and engineering, has also produced recommendations on the implementation of small groups in industry. According to a 1990 survey carried out by the Deutsche Quality Circle-Gesellschaft e.V., some 50 per cent of the largest industrial companies (by turnover) in West Germany operate quality circles, with a further 11 per cent planning to introduce them.

From being suspicious of many aspects of the 'new industrial relations' some German unions, and most notably the largest, IG Metall, have begun to extend acceptance based on the prospect of greater rights over control and working environment issues being delegated to the shop floor. In this respect, ideas of group working, quality control, and enhanced training and development, accord with features of German industrial culture and traditional labour movement concepts of workplace co-determination and participation. Motions were passed at IG Metall conferences in 1986 and 1989 calling for the exploration of team working, on a trade union agenda, as a means of reducing the monotony and excessive specialization characteristic of mass production organized on Taylorist lines. IG Metall's bargaining agenda for the 1990s, 'Tarifreform 2000', also includes proposals for exploring how new industrial relations practices should mesh with existing participation mechanisms.

In large firms with strong works councils team working has been introduced through negotiation, with a major agreement signed between Opel (General Motors' German subsidiary) and the metalworkers union IG Metall in April 1991. The agreement is expressly aimed both at boosting competitiveness through 'continuous improvement' and at enhancing 'individual possibilities of employee development'. Where the improved efficiency of groups means that fewer people can perform the groups' tasks, surplus members are protected against downgrading, with the possibility of transfer to higher-graded activities. It provides for weekly meetings of up to an hour, determined by the group in line with production needs, with the choice of topics also set by the group. The group can also draw on the management or works council on specific issues, which can participate in discussions. Training will be provided for all participants, with particular courses in discussion facilitation, leadership skills and conflict resolution for team leaders, group spokespeople and supervisors (*Meister*). All training schemes will be discussed with the works council, and require its approval.

Employee participation at board level

General principles

Work-force participation at board level is limited according to the size of the company, the company's legal form, and the industry. The main provisions are outlined below for each of the three basic systems. Although consideration has occasionally been given to providing a unitary system of board-level representation, there are no current proposals to do so.

Participation at board level is effected through the two-tier board structure which characterizes public joint-stock companies (*Aktiengesellschaft*, AG) incorporated under the Joint Stock Companies Act, 1965. This consists of a supervisory board (*Aufsichtsrat*) and a management board (*Vorstand*). The management board is responsible for conducting the business operations of a company, represents the enterprise legally, and is formally the employer, whereas the supervisory board is legally required to appoint the management board (in an AG) or the managing directors (in a GmbH) and oversee its/their activities. Employee representatives sit as members on the supervisory boards of companies, which meet between two and four times a year.

Given past objections to the introduction of a two-tier board system in the UK to facilitate worker directors, it is noteworthy that in Germany only joint-stock companies (AG) are required to have two boards as a matter of course. Other types of company are required to create a two-tier structure only if they are large enough to qualify for inclusion in one of the co-determination systems.

As members of the supervisory board employees have the same rights and duties as shareholder members. Trade union members are expected to transfer any directors' fees to the Hans Böckler Foundation, which researches co-determination and industrial relations issues. The supervisory board has a right to request information from the management board on all aspects of the business, and this right extends to the individual member, provided the request is supported by another member. Information which must be provided as a matter of course includes:

- Proposed corporate policies and other fundamental issues related to the management of the business.
- The profitability of the business, especially the return on equity.
- The general course of business, including sales.
- Operations which might be of considerable importance for the profitability or liquidity of the enterprise.

Considerable controversy surrounds the question of how much information employee members of the supervisory board may disclose. The law requires supervisory board members to behave with the due diligence of a manager, and not to divulge any confidential information which they acquire as a result of their activities. However, some authorities contend that this does not preclude informing works councils, who themselves are covered by confidentiality requirements.

The models

There are three forms of board-level participation:

- In joint-stock (AG) and limited liability (GmbH) companies and limited partnerships based on share capital (KgaA) with more than 2,000 employees, under the 1976 Codetermination Act, the supervisory board consists of equal numbers of shareholder and employee members, with the size of board varying according to company size. Some seats on the employee side are reserved for the representatives of trade unions which have members in the enterprise. The remaining seats are allocated to employees, with a guarantee of at least one seat for blue-collar, white-collar and managerial employees. Election is usually direct, by employee groups, in enterprises with up to 8,000 employees, and by electoral college in larger firms. About 520 companies are covered by the Act.

  The most important single activity of the supervisory board is to elect the management board. In this the chair of the board, who is a shareholders' representative, has a casting vote in the event of a tie. (The deputy chair is an employees' representative.) The fifty–fifty composition of the board is also weakened, from the trade union point of view, by the presence of managerial staff on the employees' side, who might typically be expected to support shareholders' views on major issues. The board also elects to the management board a so-called labour director with special responsibility for personnel and social matters: although the employee side has no veto over the appointment (see below), this manager is expected to enjoy the confidence of employee members.

- In enterprises with more than 1,000 employees engaged in the coal, iron and steel industries (the so-called 'Montan' industries), under the 1951 Montan Codetermination Act, broadly extended in 1956 to holding companies controlling enterprises in these industries, the supervisory board consists of an equal number of employee and shareholder representatives. The difference from the 1976 Act is that the chair must be a neutral member, and the labour director cannot be appointed against the wishes of the employee representatives. (Deadlock is very rare, however).

  The number of companies covered by the Act has fallen from around 100 at its inception to about thirty now. A succession of statutory interventions has taken place, designed to maintain the system in the face of the decline in these basic industries – reflected in the diminishing share of the turnover of many companies and conglomerates accounted for by these operations below the 50 per cent required under the law. In 1981 a law ruled that any company which no longer met this criterion would remain covered by the Act for a period of six years thereafter. In 1988 a new amendment was passed which provided for the controlling companies in industrial groups to remain within the scope of the Act as long as 20 per cent of their turnover was accounted for by these industries, or the subsidiary active in the industries employed at least 2,000 workers. (In practice, most individual companies which fell outside the scope of the Act in the past did so through merger or complete abandonment of this type of activity: hence the recent legislation focuses on the nature of the controlling groups in conglomerates rather than individual enterprises.)

- In companies with between 500 and 2,000 employees, under the 1952 Works Constitution Act (the predecessor to the 1972 Act but still applicable in this area), one third of the members of the supervisory board must be employee representatives.

Trade unions

Trade union structure

There are four union centres in Germany, of which by far the most important is the German Trade Union Federation (Deutscher Gewerksschaftsbund, DGB), established as a non-political centre based on industrial unionism in 1949. Although the overwhelming support of most of the DGB goes to the Social Democrats, its political independence – a product of the political divisions seen in the latter years of the Weimar Republic – is symbolized by the fact that the deputy general secretary is traditionally a member of the Christian Democrats. In 1989 the DGB had a membership in West Germany of some 7,860,000 and accounted for 97 per cent of all blue-collar and 75 per cent of all white-collar union members. The sixteen unions within the DGB are organized on an industry basis – that is, they represent all employees, both blue and white-collar, within one individual industry or sector. The DGB does not itself conduct collective bargaining.

The German Salaried Employees' Trade Union (Deutsche Angestellten-Gewerkschaft, DAG) represents white-collar employees across industry boundaries, and in 1989 had some 500,000 members. It negotiates direct with employers, although where other unions are represented there will ultimately be only one collective agreement covering an industry or enterprise. There has recently been a renewed wave of discussion about the possibility of a merger between the DAG and the DGB's commerce and finance affiliate, the HBV.

The Christian Trade Union Federation (Christlicher Gewerkschaftsbund, CGB) has 300,000 members.

The German Civil Servants' Federation (Deutscher Beamtenbund, DBB), represents established civil servants (*Beamte*) and had approximately 790,000 members in 1989: however, civil servants' pay is set by the government, not collectively bargained, and civil servants are forbidden to strike: hence, for reasons set out below, the DBB is not deemed competent to negotiate and enter into collective agreements.

Union density

These four organizations – the DGB, CGCB, DAG and DBB – had a total combined membership at the end of 1989 of 9,462,000, equivalent to 38·5 per cent of the overall West German work force. Of this total, 32 per cent of all employees are organized in DGB-affiliated unions, 3·2 per cent in the DBB, 2 per cent in the DAG and 1·2 per cent in the CGB. Some 50 per cent of all manual workers are trade union members, of whom 97 per cent are in DGB unions: 21 per cent of white-collar employees are in unions, of whom 74 per cent are in DGB unions and 20 per cent in the DAG.

German trade unions have not experienced the major collapses or erosion of membership seen elsewhere: total membership of the DGB in West Germany rose from 7,660,000 in 1984 to 7,861,000 in 1989. However, trade union density (DGB-affiliated) peaked at 34·2 per cent of the work force in 1978. Certain unions, such as IG Metall in metalworking, the public-sector union ÖTV and the commerce union HBV have been able to increase their membership during the 1980s. (Following German unification and the dissolution of the former Communist union centre, the FDGB, East German industrial unions have joined the West German counterparts, substantially increasing the overall size of DGB unions. Participation has remained generally high.)

The average rates of union density cited above mask substantial variations. Whereas 85–90 per cent of workers in large engineering works may be union members, union organization is low in the private service sector and in industries such as electronics. There is also underrepresentation of women, and a fall has been recorded in the number of young people joining trade unions.

Membership of a trade union is entirely voluntary, and dues are relatively high compared to the UK, with members paying about 1 per cent of gross pay. The DGB is financed by 12 per cent of each affiliated union's dues, and runs its own research institute, the WSI, based in Düsseldorf.

The Union der Leitenden Angestellten (ULA) represents senior executives and managerial staff but has no role in pay determination. The terms and conditions of such employees are laid down in individual contracts of employment or unilaterally determined company scales, so the ULA does not bargain on their behalf but represents their interests. (It has about 40,000 members.)

Freedom of association

The right to form and join a trades union (or employers' association) is guaranteed under the 1949 Basic Law, which grants 'The right to form associations to safeguard and improve working and economic conditions . . . to everyone and to all trades, occupations and professions'. Any agreement which seeks to limit this right is null and void. The principle has also been interpreted by the courts as meaning that individuals also have a right not to belong to a trade union: the closed shop is therefore illegal.

Trade unions have a right to carry out recruitment activities at the workplace by distributing trade union literature outside working hours, and by using any notice boards intended to inform employees. However, there is no guaranteed right, for example, to hold shop stewards' elections at the workplace should the employer refuse.

The courts have developed the principles embodied in the Basic Law into a body of case law on what type of organization can legitimately claim to be an association, enjoy constitutional protection, and participate in collective bargaining. These principles apply equally to both employee and employer organizations. They include:

- The association must be a voluntary organization and must, in general, operate above the level of the individual enterprise or establishment.
- It must constitute a genuine opposition to its counterpart, and
, be organizationally independent of it and the state.
- It must fulfil certain minimum standards of democracy.
- The association must be prepared to acknowledge and respect the law on collective bargaining, and have as its objective the conclusion of collective agreements.
- It must be both willing and able to back up its demands with the exercise of collective pressure in the form of strikes or lock-outs: the courts have, for example, ruled that employee organizations that are too small or not regarded seriously by employers cannot command the competence to sign collective agreements.

Employers' organizations

Employers' associations are organized along industrial lines on a regional basis, with a national centre, the Confederation of German Employers' Associations (Bundesvereinigung der deutschen Arbeitgeberverbände, BDA), which embraces some 700 employers' organizations represented through forty-six industry and twelve regional groups. Like the DGB, the BDA itself does not conclude collective agreements; this is done by the national or regional industrial affiliates. Member organizations of the BDA generally have a high degree of representativeness of employers in their industries. For example, some 75 per cent of all employees in the metalworking industry work in firms affiliated to the Metal Trades Employers' Associations (whose central federation is Gesamtmetall).

Although the BDA does not negotiate, and lacks formal central powers, it exercises considerable sway over the conduct of industry negotiations, which some commentators hold to have increased over the last two to three decades. The BDA's annual report customarily features a section on 'co-ordination of bargaining' in which the federation's views on the coming pay round are set out, reflecting the discussions held in the BDA's Pay and Collective Bargaining Committee. However, the BDA does not publicly set out specific pay recommendations, although once the pay round has begun settlements tend to converge around a narrow 'going rate'.

Despite this attempt at co-ordination, it is the industry associations – which are coalitions of businesses of various types and interests – which undertake the actual bargaining, and the BDA's 'line' can be weakened or partly abandoned during negotiations. Tensions can also develop within industry associations between the interests of smaller and larger concerns, between regions, and between the central organizations and the regional bodies on which local employers are directly represented, and usually become most evident during a difficult pay round. In general, however, the need to retain marginal firms in industry organizations and confront generally strong industrial unions enforces both discipline and a broad averaging of interests.

Bargaining

The right to form trade unions and employers' associations, to bargain collectively, and to back up bargaining by industrial action, are rights derived from the founding constitution of the Federal Republic, the 1949 Basic Law. The law on industrial action has been developed by the courts on the basis of the argument that collective bargaining by trade unions would be 'collective begging' without a right to exercise forms of collective pressure. (Slightly different principles were applied to the employers' right to lock out; see below). The right to take industrial action to back claims up is one important line of legal demarcation in the German system between 'collective bargaining' in the narrow sense (termed *Tarifverhandlung*), in which employees' interests are represented by trade unions, and the statutory systems of employee representation outlined above.

Collective bargaining can take place only between trade unions and individual employers or employers' associations. Collective bargaining culminates in the conclusion of a collective agreement (*Tarifvertrag*), which is legally binding and typically includes a clause forbidding any industrial action during the life of the agreement and for a period thereafter. Collective agreements can also apply to non-signatory employers through ministerial extension.

Collective agreements negotiated between employers and trade unions take precedence over other forms of industrial accord, such as works agreements (see above) or individual contracts, unless these diverge in favour of the employee.

Basic provisions on pay, grading systems, working hours and holidays, premium pay rates and many other general terms of employment for the vast majority of employees are established by industry-level collective agreements agreed at regional or national level between trade unions and employers' organizations. That is, most bargaining on pay is removed from the workplace, an important feature stressed by practitioners on both sides of industry as removing a good deal of 'potential for conflict' from the workplace, leaving workplace systems of consultation and negotiation to deal with more 'qualitative' issues.

There are a total of approximately 800 bargaining units – that is, regional/industrial areas – at which agreements are signed between unions and employers' associations. (Bargaining between a trade union and an individual company on basic pay affects comparatively few employees.) Volkswagen, the oil companies and some firms in publishing are the major examples of employers which negotiate on basic terms direct with trade unions.) Of these 800, however, only a relatively small number set the terms of employment for a large proportion of the German work force, and an even smaller number shape the bargaining environment in the pay round (see the fourth European Management Guide, on pay).

In the former Federal Republic collective agreements, either directly or indirectly, cover industries employing around 90 per cent of the total work force. Indirectly, in this context, means that employers who are not members of employers' associations frequently adopt the essential provisions of the agreement regulating the industry they are in. The only areas not covered are those with employers who do not traditionally have collective pay setting, such as lawyers' chambers. Around a quarter of the covered work force – 4·5 million employees – are protected by collective agreements which have been extended by ministerial decree to employees of non-signatory firms. The system of legally enforceable and extendable collective agreements constitutes the mechanism for guaranteeing minimum conditions and pay levels in Germany. There is no statutory minimum wage. In practice, most extended agreements cover issues other than pay, with only about 700,000 of the 4·5 million employees concerned subject to extended pay provisions.

Although, in formal terms, most collective agreements are regional, there is a high degree of centralization within trade unions and employers' organizations. National executives will oversee what their regional officials are doing, and may centralize the negotiating process if there is a block at regional level or a divergence from the national policy. (In formal terms, one region may still be the pacesetter for the industry, as the agreement will have to be signed by the regional industrial employers' organization and the regional officials of the union.) Minimum pay rates may vary a little from region to region, but most other terms will be common to all regions.

Despite the relatively high degree of centralization in the system, around 5,000 collective agreements are agreed annually (in West Germany), of which 3,000 are between unions and employers' associations, and 2,000 between unions and companies. Most of these replace expiring agreements. Around 25,000 agreements in total were in force in 1990. The main reason for the large number is that each region/industry or firm is covered by several agreements, each of which regulates a different area of terms and conditions. Provisions on issues such as working hours, leave, premium rates, notice and probationary periods are set by so-called 'framework agreements', which typically remain in force for several years. Pay levels for each grade are set by a separate pay agreement, revised in each pay round. Grading, training, early retirement, 'rationalization protection', saving schemes (so-called 'capital formation') may also all be settled by a specific agreement.

Industrial conflict

The law on industrial action is virtually wholly developed on the basis of court interpretations of the constitutional guarantee of freedom of association noted above. This sanctions both strikes and lock-outs, subject to a number of criteria. Striking suspends and does not breach the individual contract of employment and does not, therefore, provide grounds for dismissal, provided the action is lawful.

Freedom to take industrial action is, in the first instance, constrained by peace clauses in collective agreements which forbid industrial action during the lifetime of an agreement and for a period thereafter. In the metalworking industry procedure agreement this extends for four weeks after the agreement expires. In the chemical industry the parties bind themselves not to undertake industrial action until conciliation machinery has been exhausted. A peace obligation is deemed to be an implicit term of collective agreements as regards disputes of rights, although agreements may also contain a written commitment to refrain from all forms of action. Separate agreed conciliation and arbitration arrangements usually exist for disputes of rights, arising out of interpretation of a current agreement, and disputes of interests arising out of negotiations for a new collective agreement (or renewal of an expired one). There is no compulsory state arbitration service.

In the metalworking industry, disputes of rights are dealt with by a disputes procedure set out in the industry's regional framework agreements. Problems are initially handled by managements and works councils, and may be referred to the employers' organization and the trade union in the event of failure to agree. Should even these two signatories fail to agree, the issue will be referred to a standing arbitration committee, which consists of two representatives from each side plus an independent chair nominated by both sides (or appointed by the President of the *Land* labour court in the event of disagreement). The committee then issues a binding ruling which is final – with no recourse to law. The typical procedure for conciliation during pay bargaining will be considered in Volume 4 of the European Management Guides, on pay determination.

Strikes

In general, full-scale strikes are permissible only once negotiations have broken down, and one of the parties has formally declared as much; that is, a strike must be the last resort (*ultima ratio* principle). The issue of token strikes of short duration during negotiations – termed 'warning strikes' (*Warnstreik*) in German – is more complex, and there are still differences of opinion over how to interpret the Federal Labour Court's most recent judgement on the subject in 1988. In 1976 such strikes were declared legal provided they were called by a trade union and did not violate a peace clause, thus relaxing the 'last resort' principle. Trade union officials can usually call such strikes without the need for a ballot (see below). The development of flexible tactics of industrial action by unions such as IG Metall in the 1980s, in which selective short stoppages would be combined with demonstrations, led to employer challenges to the 1976 ruling. In 1988 the Federal Labour Court appeared to reverse its judgement by stating that token strikes did not enjoy any privilege compared with other forms of industrial action and had to remain a last resort. However, it also stated that no formal declaration of a breakdown of talks was necessary to make such action lawful; rather, the possibility of negotiations had to be 'exhausted'. Whether such a situation had arrived was expressly left by the ruling to the judgement of the trade union. In practice, token strikes are a frequent accompaniment to negotiations in Germany.

For a full scale strike to be lawful:

- It must be the last resort, and be proportional to its objectives, 'fairly conducted' and must not seek the destruction of the opponent.

- It must be called by a trade union: 'wildcat' strikes are unlawful. Strikes are therefore subject to the balloting requirements in the constitutions of trade unions which typically require a 75 per cent vote in favour of any proposed action. However, a union can subsequently legitimate an unofficial strike.
- It must have as its aim matters which can be regulated in a collective agreement. That is, a political strike aimed at exerting pressure on the legislature would be unlawful. Opinions differ on the lawfulness of sympathy action: while some authorities claim that such action is unlawful, as the employees concerned would not be seeking to affect their own terms and conditions, some court rulings appear to uphold sympathy action in support of a lawful strike in another region, or where the employer may not be wholly disinterested in the outcome.

Unions, though only rarely individuals, have been fined for engaging in unlawful industrial action.

Lock-outs

Lock-outs are lawful, subject to certain conditions, and have featured in industrial disputes, notably in printing and metal-working. The most recent case law on lock-outs was developed in the context of the extent to which employers could respond to a series of official but selective strikes. That is, where the trade union was concerned to keep strike action as selective as possible, the employers had a legitimate interest in widening it so as to impose additional costs on the union in the form of strike pay. In its 1980 judgement the Federal Labour Court upheld the lawfulness of lock-outs but set out a series of criteria which they needed to meet in order to achieve a fair balance between trade union and employer power. Lock-outs must:

- Fulfil the 'last resort' requirement, and not aim at the destruction of the other party.
- Be confined to the collective bargaining region in which the dispute is taking place.
- Be proportional to the trade union action. This was quantified by the court in the following terms: if fewer than 25 per cent of the employees in a region are on strike, then the employers'

side may lock out a further 25 per cent of the relevant work force; if more than 25 per cent of the work force are on strike, the employer may lock workers out, provided no more than 50 per cent of the workers in a region are either on strike or locked out.

Strike pay and unemployment benefit

Strike pay, usually worth around two-thirds of previous earnings, is paid in the event of official disputes to workers directly engaged in industrial action. Under a new ruling in January 1991 the Federal Income Appeal Tribunal ruled that strike pay is tax-free.

Strikers cannot claim unemployment benefit. However, the issue of whether unemployment or short-time benefit may be paid to workers laid off as a result of action elsewhere caused a major controversy in the 1980s, led the government to change the law in this regard in 1986, and remains a contentious topic. The change, which restricted access to unemployment benefits, followed the six-week strike over shorter hours in the engineering industry, in which the IG Metall union used selective action in some regions to hit vulnerable supply chains in the car industry, relying on firms outside regions in which it was organizing strikes to lay workers off on unemployment benefit, avoiding the need for strike pay, and putting pressure on the employers' side in the negotiations.

Under the 1969 Work Promotion Act, as amended, workers affected by temporary lay-offs as a result of a strike in another collective bargaining region are not entitled to unemployment benefit if they work in the same industry, and *if* the union's demands in their region are 'equivalent in scale and character' to those in the region on strike (although they do not have to be identical to them) *and* if the outcome of bargaining in the region on strike would be adopted in substance by the affected region. The new provisions have not been tested as yet in the metalworking industry, as bargaining rounds since 1986 (1987, 1990, 1991) have passed off without a full-scale strike.

Collective dismissal

German law requires that redundancies represent a 'last resort', and employers must examine whether they could be avoided by the introduction of short-time working, reducing overtime, internal transfer of employees, or other measures, most of which require consultation with the works council. In making employees redundant, employers must also ensure that the choice of employee meets a set of 'social criteria', and that employees dismissed must be those least 'socially affected'. Works councils and employers can agree on a points system of selection for redundancy, but must take into account length of service, age and number of dependants, with the possibility of helping individual cases of hardship.

Notification procedure

Notification and consultation procedures depend on the number of proposed redundancies and the size of the establishment.

In all establishments with more than twenty employees the employer must inform the works council of any changes in the running of the establishment which might entail 'substantial disadvantages' for the work force (see above). Once they are decided on, and as with any dismissal, the works council must also be notified irrespective of the number of redundancies. And as with individual dismissals, the works council can either express reservations about the proposed dismissal, agree to it (implicitly, by not responding to the proposal within the required period) or object to it. (See the second volume in the series European Management Guides, *Terms and Conditions of Employment*, pp. 86–90.)

Under the 1969 Work Promotion Act, employers must notify the *Land* labour office (*Landesarbeitsamt*) if they envisage any changes in the running of the establishment which *might* lead to collective redundancies occurring within the next twelve months. The opinion of the works council must be appended to the notification. A collective redundancy is defined in the 1969 Protection against Dismissals Act as the dismissal on economic grounds within thirty calendar days of:

- More than five employees in an establishment employing more than twenty and fewer than sixty employees.
- More than twenty-five employees or 10 per cent of those

regularly employed in establishments with at least sixty and
fewer than 500 employees.
- At least thirty employees in an establishment employing more
than 500 employees.

Once the employer makes a decision to proceed with redundancies, the works council must be informed 'in good time and in
writing of the reason for the proposed redundancies, the number
of employees to be dismissed, the number of employees usually
employed and the period of time over which the redundancies
are to take place'. Other 'appropriate information' should be
also attached. The works council should be informed at least
two weeks before the employer carries out the required notification
of the local labour office (*Arbeitsamt*).

Notification of the local labour office must include the information supplied to the works council as well as the works
council's comments. If no opinion from the works council is
available, the dismissal will be valid if the employer can prove
that they informed the works council at least two weeks before
submitting the notification to the labour office. The notification
must include:

- The name of the employer, registered office, and nature of the
business.
- The number of employees usually employed, the proposed
number of redundancies and the reasons for the dismissals.
- The period over which the redundancies are to be effected.

Where the works council gives its permission, the notification
may also include information about the sex, age, occupation and
nationality of the employees to be made redundant, to assist in
placement or training.

There is a normal minimum of one month between the submission
of the notification and the date from which dismissals can be
effective. This period can be reduced only with the permission of
the labour office. The labour office can also decide that a further
month should elapse before dismissals become effective. Failure
to supply the required notification will make the redundancy
invalid. However, a collective redundancy does not require the
authorization of the labour office.

'Reconciliation of interests'

In the first instance, and after informing the works council about proposed changes in the running of the establishment, and before proceeding with any dismissals, the employer has to seek to come to an agreement with the works council on how and when the changes are to be implemented. The agreement should be set out in writing, and is termed a 'reconciliation of interests' (*Interessenausgleich*). The works council has no enforceable right of co-determination at this stage, as it is regarded as an operational decision which lies within management's prerogative. In certain circumstances, however, the works council has an enforceable right of co-determination over the establishment of a social compensation plan (*Sozialplan*) to provide for severance payments and other assistance to those dismissed (see below).

Redundancy payments

There is no statutory obligation on employers to make payments for redundancy over and above normal pay during notice. However, provision for a redundancy payment may be included in a collective agreement, an individual contract of employment or a works agreement as part of a social compensation plan. Where redundancy pay is provided for, it is often calculated on the same basis as compensation for unfair dismissal: that is, one month's salary for each year of service, up to twelve years', with more for older employees. (However, many collective agreements provide guarantees against redundancy for employees over 55, who can be dismissed only for serious misconduct.)

Social compensation plans provide probably the most common means by which employees receive payments in the event of redundancy. They take the form of a works agreement (see above). Under certain circumstances, works councils have an enforceable right to negotiate a social plan, and to obtain a binding ruling from a conciliation committee if no agreement can be reached with the employer. In giving a ruling the committee is obliged, in broad terms, to consider the 'social interests' of the affected employees and the 'economic reasonableness' of its decision for the undertaking. Section 112 of the 1972 Works Constitution Act sets out more specific guidelines:

- The award should be appropriate to the individual circumstances of individual employees (that is, no across-the-board awards), especially where the question of lost service or pension entitlements is concerned.
- The award should pay due regard to the prospects of dismissed employees on the labour market. Employees should be excluded from the scope of a plan if they can be employed in a 'reasonable' post in the same establishment or another establishment of the same enterprise or if they refuse such employment. The fact that another establishment is not in the same location as their existing employment does not in itself make the offer of employment unreasonable (see below).
- The conciliation committee must ensure that the overall scale of payments made under a plan does not prejudice the continued existence of the plant or jeopardize any remaining employment in the establishment.

An amendment to section 112 of the Works Constitution Act, introduced through the Employment Promotion Act, 1985, laid down new and more restrictive conditions, under which a social plan may be obligatory. Under the 1985 rules a social plan is obligatory only when it is planned to make redundant the following percentage *and* number of employees, including those who leave because of the change in the establishment on the basis of a termination by mutual consent.

No. of employees in establishment	Percentage to be dismissed	Minimum No. to be dismissed
21–59	20	at least 6
60–249	20	at least 37
250–499	15	at least 60
499–	10	at least 60

A works council cannot enforce a social plan in any enterprise in the first four years after its establishment. However, this does not apply in the case of companies which set up as a result of a restructuring of an existing enterprise or group (*Konzern*). It does not remove the obligation to attempt a 'reconciliation of interests' with the works council, irrespective of how long the firm has existed.

Social plans can make provisions in a variety of areas, including:

- Severance payment.
- Loans to employees.
- Help with finding new employment ('outplacement'), together with time off and fares.
- Extra hardship provisions.
- Payment of any anniversary payments due.
- Removal costs where appropriate.
- Entitlement to leave and holiday bonus.
- Continued payment of capital formation payments under the German SAYE scheme.

Payments under a social plan will be exempted from income tax, subject to an upper limit of DM 24,000 (£8,135) rising to DM 36,000 (£12,200) for older employees with long service.

Transfer of undertakings

The transfer of ownership of undertakings is regulated by Section 613(a) of the Civil Code, intended to give effect to EC Directive 77/187 on acquired rights. Work-force consultation is not specifically provided for in the Civil Code. However, the 1972 Works Constitution Act (Section 111) already requires works councils in establishments with more than 20 employees to be informed of any changes with possible disadvantageous consequences for the work force, and Section 106 of the 1972 Act (which applies in undertakings with more than 100 employees) provides for extensive information to be provided on any plans which might impinge on the interests of the work force.

The German Basic Law also provides for the individual employee to exercise a right of objection to a new employer, and to choose to continue to be employed by their former employer – albeit at risk of redundancy: in order for this right to be realized, the transferor is implicitly obliged, specifically in the absence of a works council, to inform employees of the proposed change, in line with the consultation requirements of Article 6 of the EC Directive.

No regulations have been issued to clarify how EC law and German law are to be put into effect, and this has caused problems in the interpretation of the provisions. Controversy has also been caused by the decision of the German government to set aside the operation of Section 613(a) in the former GDR until the end of 1992 in order to ease the transfer and privatization of former state-owned undertakings.

Specifically, the law requires that:

* In the event of a transfer, the transferor assumes the rights and obligations arising out of the employment relationships existing at the time of the transfer. If these rights and obligations are regulated by a collective or works agreement, then these provisions become part of employees' individual contracts of employment and may not be altered to their disadvantage until a year has elapsed. This does not apply if the rights and norms of employees at the new employer are regulated by a different collective or works agreement.

* The transfer in itself may not be used as grounds for termination (even for employees who would not otherwise be covered by dismissal protection legislation, such as those in small firms or with less than six months' service). However, termination on other grounds, such as genuine redundancy, is not precluded: there is a substantial body of case law elucidating where the transfer itself has legitimately provided the principal motive for dismissal, and identifying instances in which the courts ruled that employers have sought to circumvent the law.

Appendix

The Federal Ministry of Labour
(Bundesministerium für Arbeit
und Sozialordnung):
5300 Bonn 1
Postfach 14 02 80
Rochustrasse 1
tel. + 49 228 5271

Federal Employment Institute
(Bundesanstalt für Arbeit, BfA):
Regensburgerstrasse 104
8500 Nürnberg 30
tel. + 49 911 171
fax + 49 911 17 21 23

Federal Association of German
Management Consultants
(Bundesverband Deutscher
Unternehmensberater, BDU eV):
Friedrich-Wilhelm-Strasse 2
5300 Bonn 1
tel. + 49 228 23 80 55
fax + 49 228 23 06 25

British Chamber of Commerce in
Germany:
Heumarkt 14
5000 Köln 1
tel. + 49 221 234284

Confederation of German
Employers' Associations (BDA)
Gustav Heinemann Ufer 72
5000 Köln 51
tel. + 49 221 37950
fax + 49 221 3795 235

Gesamtmetall (Federation of
Metal Trades Employers'
Associations):
Volksgartenstrasse 54a
Postfach 25 01 25
5000 Köln
tel. + 49 221 33 99 0
fax + 49 221 33 99 233

Bundesarbeitgeberverband
Chemie e.V. (chemical industry
employers' association):
Abraham-Lincoln-Strasse 24
6200 Wiesbaden
tel. + 49 611 71 90 16
fax + 49 611 71 90 10

German Society for Personnel
Management (Deutsche
Gesellschaft für
Personalführung e.V. DGFP):
4000 Düsseldorf 1
Niederkasseler Lohweg 16
tel. + 49 211 59 78 0
fax + 49 211 59 78 505

German Trade Union
Confederation (Deutscher
Gewerkschaftsbund, DGB):
Hans-Böckler-Haus
Hans-Böckler-Strasse 39
4000 Düsseldorf 30
tel. + 49 211 43010
fax + 49 211 43 01471

Union der Leitenden
Angestellten (ULA):
Alfredstrasse 77–9
4300 Essen 1
tel. + 49 201 78 20 35–6
fax + 49 201 78 72 08

5

Greece

Trade union activity in Greece was heavily restricted during the dictatorships of 1936–41 and 1967–74, it went completely underground during the foreign occupation in 1941–45, and it was allowed only for non-communists during the 1945–67 period, when the Communist Party of Greece (KKE) was outlawed. Free industrial relations have applied since the restoration of democracy and the legalization of the Communist Party in 1974.

Industrial relations are based on the 1975 constitution, which grants basic trade union freedoms, on legislation – in particular the 1982 law on union organization and industrial action and the 1990 law on collective bargaining – and on collective agreements.

Although the full development of free collective bargaining has been held back by the marked intervention of the state in the form of compulsory arbitration and weaknesses in trade union organization at national level, there are hopes that legislation passed in 1990 will foster greater autonomy in negotiations and normalization of relationships between employers and trade unions. In particular, conciliation, mediation and arbitration procedures have been introduced with the aim of avoiding the compulsory intervention of the state in the bargaining process.

Under the 1990 agreement between the main union centre, GSEE, and the main employers association, SEB, provision was made for joint consideration of major national economic issues, such as employment growth, productivity, industrial relations and training, to lay the basis for more detailed studies and appropriate responses. This followed a national agreement on joint health and safety discussions, concluded in 1989.

Statutory and agreed mechanisms for employee participation

Employees are represented at the workplace through local trade union organizations (see below), works councils, and health and safety committees.

Works councils

Greek legislation on works councils in accord with International Agreement 135, approved in 1971 at the fifty-sixth ILO Conference, was introduced in 1988.

The Act specifies that employees in enterprises with at least fifty employees, or with between twenty and fifty employees if there is a workplace trade union, have the right to elect work councils in a general assembly of all employees, at the place of work or elsewhere. ('Enterprise' here also refers to branches or separate operations of a company). The management and the relevant trade unions must be notified of the election. The law does not cover socialized enterprises (see below) and shipping companies.

The size of the council varies in accordance with the number of employees in the enterprise, with three members in firms with fewer than 300 employees, five in those with 301–1,000 and seven in firms with over 1,000 employees. During their two-year term of office members enjoy the protection granted to union officials by law 1264 of 1982. The chair of the council can have two hours' a week paid leave of absence in order to carry out their duties. Works council members have a right to twelve days per term of office in order to attend training programmes organized by the relevant top-level trade union organization (see below). The cost of operating the system, including the provision of office space, is borne by the employer.

The function of works councils is 'participatory and consultative', and they are not intended to prejudice or displace trade unions, whose bargaining role to safeguard employee interests is expressly recognized in the 1988 law. Councils are required to co-operate with unions and provide them with any information which falls within their competence. However, agreements between works councils and managements do not bind the unions in their pay or other claims.

Councils may not act in ways which cause harm to the firm. They should confer with management at least once every two months, and managements must provide the information necessary, together with any other reasonable help, for them to carry out their duties.

The information to be given and the observance of confidentiality by council members are specified in detail by law. The information includes:

- Any change in the legal state of the enterprise.
- A total or partial transfer, expansion or reduction of its installations.
- The introduction of new technology.
- Changes in staff organization, a reduction or increase in the number of employees, proposed overtime and any lay-offs or rotation of workers.
- Annual plans for investment in health and safety.
- Business plans, balance sheets and accounts, the scheduling of production.

Works councils may also jointly decide a number of issues where these are not already regulated by collective agreement or where there is no trade union organization in the enterprise. They include:

- Internal works rules.
- Health and safety rules.
- The scheduling of training.
- Cultural activities.

The works council is also the body which employers must consult over collective dismissals if no trade union organization exists at the workplace (see also below).

Works councils have not yet made any substantial progress, and considerable trade union suspicion remains about the new institutions. Given the relative novelty of the legislation, however, it is too early to attempt an overall assessment. Employee involvement also takes place on an agreed basis in a small number of generally large firms.

Health and safety committees

Law 1568, passed in 1985, makes provision for the establishment of health and safety committees, consisting solely of employees, in all private companies with more than fifty employees. In enterprises with between twenty and fifty employees, workers elect a single representative.

The size of the committee varies from two members (51–100 employees) to seven in enterprises with more than 2,000 employees. The committees consult the employer on health and safety issues, and members are entitled to time off for training.

Board-level participation

Legislation dating from 1983 provides for the establishment of a two-tier board structure, with scope for employee representatives to sit on supervisory boards. In Greece supervisory boards do not have the power to appoint the management board. However, the system appears to be little used.

Participation in public enterprises

Law 1365/1983, for the 'Socialization of Public Enterprises and Utilities', introduced the participation of interested parties, including employees and local authorities, in the planning and management of all state enterprises. Specifically, the 'social supervisory boards' of public and state enterprises must consist of equal numbers of representatives of employees, local authorities, and consumer and other organizations directly affected by the enterprise. The supervisory board has extensive powers, including proposing long-term plans, examining and approving the annual report and accounts, appointing auditors, and offering advice on the establishment of subsidiaries. Public enterprises also have a management board, consisting of nine members, three of whom are elected by the work force: the management board is responsible for the management and legal representation of the enterprise. Public enterprises must also establish a central works council, with nine members, which has an advisory role.

Public enterprises in Greece are more numerous and engaged in more branches of industry, including transport and banking, than the public sector is in most other EC countries, and estimated to account for over 50 per cent of total gross domestic product. The Liberal government elected in April 1990 has declared its intention of proceeding with large-scale deregulation and privatization of the state sector.

Experience with the system has not generally been positive. Introduced by the then Socialist majority in Parliament, it was opposed by the Liberals because of anxieties that it might spill over to the private sector of the economy. On the other hand, the Communist Party and some trade unionists regarded it as an attempt to conceal the real conflict between labour and management.

Trade unions

Greek trade unionism presents a complex and sometimes less than transparent picture, mainly because of the proliferation of 'primary' unions, allowed under union legislation, many of which exist in name only, having been originally established to obtain representation on political grounds in higher representative structures. There are three tiers of trade unions:

- 'Primary trade unions', which exist at local area level or on an establishment basis.
- 'Secondary trade union organizations', consisting of either federations of at least two primary unions, or regional labour centres.
- 'Tertiary trade union organizations', the confederations, which consist of associations of federations and labour centres. The central confederation, deemed competent to bargain and representative of most organized workers, is GSEE, the Greek General Confederation of Labour.

Trade union rights and freedoms, internal union democracy and administrative regulations, together with the law on industrial action, are regulated by law 1264, passed in 1982. The Act, for example, closely regulates the procedures by which delegates from lower tiers of trade union organization are elected to higher tiers. One aim behind the law was to counter the tendency towards the proliferation of unions seen since the mid-1970s, by restricting direct representation of primary unions to the secondary level: primary unions are not directly represented in the GSEE, but only through federations and labour centres.

A minimum number of twenty-one persons can apply formally to the court to form a union. Legal status is acquired upon the (almost certain) approval of the court.

Basic trade union rights

Employers may not hamper trade union organization, require employees to join or not to join a particular union, or intervene in the administration of unions. Nor may they support unions financially, unless the expenditure is deemed to support socially beneficial goals for primary trade unions. The 1982 law created the basis of independent trade union financing by allowing voluntary dues collection, by check-off if agreed, to replace the system based on compulsory dues levied through the social insurance system (Workers' Hearth) and distributed to unions on the basis of membership, which includes an employer contribution. (This system will end on 1 January 1992 under law 1915, passed on 28 December 1990.)

Termination of contract on grounds of trade union activity is invalid, and trade union officials and members of trade union executives enjoy protection against dismissal during the period of office and for a year thereafter. The number of protected employees depends on the size of the union. However, dismissal is possible on grounds of serious misconduct, such as disclosure of company secrets, physical injury or serious insult to the employer or their representative, persistent refusal to carry out contractual obligations at work, or unauthorized absence.

Trade union officials have the right to extra leave of absence, and to reduced working time, the amount of time off depending on the nature of the office held. Primary unions at the workplace are entitled to notice boards and, if there are more than 100 employees, to suitable office space for the most representative union in the establishment.

By law management must recognize all unions functioning in the firm. They negotiate, however, with the union having most members or the most representative one. The Ministry of Labour and often the courts are involved in determining which union is the most representative. The union considered most representative is the one deemed best able to keep the terms of a collective agreement (see also below). Frequently, however, separate agreements are made with two similar unions, allowing the possibility of employees in the same firm doing the same work at different rates of pay because their respective unions have agreed different pay rates.

Structure and membership

The primary unions, most of which are craft-based, are numerous: around 2,400 are estimated to be active. They are organized into about seventy-seven federations and eighty-four regional labour centres, and these in turn are affiliated to the GSEE. The forty-five members of the executive committee of the GSEE are elected by representatives of the federations and the labour centres at the Labour Congress, held every two or three years, and belong to all political tendencies. They have a distinct political identity and platform. There are three other private-sector confederations, but they do not command sufficient membership or standing to be regarded as of significance in the industrial relations system.

The unions for the civil servants, established in 1926, have also organized in federations, with ADEDY as their central organization. The corresponding organizations for teachers at state schools are OLME (Federation of High School Teachers) and DOE (Greek Federation of Schoolteachers).

Overall figures on union membership are imprecise. Union density among civil servants and in the public sector in general is now 70–90 per cent, two or three times higher than in the private sector of the economy. Overall density is about 35 per cent of wage and salary earners. However, this group itself represents only about half the total labour force, the lowest proportion in the European Community.

The very large number of organizations at all levels is attributable to three main factors:

- The past system of compulsory dues collection.
- The attempt by numerous political parties (thirty or more) and even more informal political groups, as well as in some cases employers, to have a means of extending their influence in the workplace.
- The background and expectations of the large majority of first-generation migrants from the rural areas, which favour small local unions.

The consequences of the large number of unions have been deleterious to the development of trade unionism. Dozens or even hundreds of unions effectively exist only on paper, detracting from the image of all unions and weakening the status of serious organizations. Many employees (technicians, drivers, engineers, doctors) are members of more than one union or professional association. The latter often follow different policies, and employers may have to deal with many unions – up to thirty-five in the case of the Public Power Corporation, for example, or more than ten in a university or a hospital.

Employers' organizations

The four main employer organizations are:

- SEB (Federation of Greek Industries).
- EEE (Union of Shipowners).
- ESE (Union of Commerce and Trade).
- GSEVE (General Confederation of Cottage Industries).

All have a dual federal structure based on branch of activity (e.g. the National Union of Textiles Industries) and on geographical area (e.g. Union of Industries in Northern Greece). By far the most influential organization is SEB, which bargains centrally with the GSEE.

Employer organizations are regulated by laws similar to those applied to the unions when the organizations consist of individual employers and by the Civic Code when they consist of associations.

Bargaining

Since the restoration of democracy and the legalization of the Communist Party in July 1974 there has been free collective bargaining, although subject to marked government intervention on occasions.

Under law 1876, passed in 1990, which introduced major changes into collective bargaining law and settlement procedures, five main levels of bargaining were established, leading to five categories of collective agreements: the clauses of collective agreements have an immediate and binding effect, whose scope depends on the specific type of agreement involved. The parties entitled to conclude collective agreements are:

- Trade unions and employee organizations at all levels within their fields of activity. National collective agreements may be signed only by 'the most representative national-level organization' – that is, the GSEE. Representativeness is determined by the number of workers who voted in the most recent elections to its governing body.
- Any employer employing at least fifty workers.

The five types of agreement specified under the 1990 law are:

- *National general* agreements (originally introduced in 1935). These agreements, which are applicable to all workers nationally without ministerial extension under the 1990 law, are concluded between tertiary-level trade unions (that is, the GSEE) and the most representative or nationwide employers' organizations. The national agreement between the GSEE and SEB sets minimum pay and general terms and conditions of employment for all employees in the private sector. (The agreement signed in March 1991 is for two years.) A second important general collective agreement is negotiated between the shipowners and the federation of seamen.
- *Sectoral* agreements, applicable in similar or related undertakings in a specific branch of industry, either nationally or in a specific locality or region. These may be signed by primary or secondary level trade union organizations (base trade union, federations or labour centres) and by industry employers' associations.
- *National occupational* agreements, negotiated between one or more national federations and one or more employers' associations of the relevant trades. Different employee categories in a firm may, therefore, be covered by different agreements.
- *Regional* agreements by craft or occupational group in a certain geographical area, concluded between labour centres and the regional associations of the employers.
- *Company* agreements, applicable in a single undertaking or

business, and concluded between the employer and an enterprise union or a primary union.

National, regional or company agreements can diverge from the terms and conditions of national general agreements only if the new terms are more favourable to the employee. Where an employment relationship is covered by several collective agreements, that most favourable to the employees will prevail, with enterprise and sectoral agreements taking precedence over occupational agreements. Non-signatory parties can accede to an agreement by private contract if they wish, although this cannot happen in the case of an enterprise agreement. The Ministry of Labour is also empowered to extend an agreement to non-signatory parties in a sector or occupation, on its own decision or by application, provided the agreement is already binding on employers employing at least 51 per cent of the workers in that sector or occupation.

Before law 1876/90 the state played a multi-faceted role in bargaining. It mediated, ratified agreements, determined minimum (and even maximum) wages and salaries by age and experience, and fixed normal working hours and severance pay. All these (except severance pay) are now determined by free collective bargaining between the parties directly concerned. (We set out the new provisions on settlement procedures in the section dealing with industrial action, below). Negotiations must be conducted in good faith, and each party must explain to the other the reasons behind its proposals or counter-proposals.

The incomes policy pursued by the government and the guidelines for maximum wage increases apply only to civil servants, teachers in state schools and to public enterprises and organizations. They influence collective bargaining in the private sector but are not a binding factor on either side. Through their separate unions civil servants and teachers in state schools negotiate with government and settle outstanding issues but do not sign collective agreements.

Industrial action

Until Feburary 1990, if bargaining failed to produce an agreement, conciliation was attempted by the Ministry of Labour. Failing that, the case went to Compulsory Arbitration of the First Instance. The decision could be appealed against to Arbitration of the Second Instance, and no strike or lock-out was allowed until a decision had been reached. The decision was binding on both sides.

Law 1876 of 1990 has replaced compulsory by voluntary arbitration and has also introduced new procedures for handling a breakdown of talks. The government still has the power to declare an emergency situation and to forbid strike activity on a national level or at any branch of activity. Both Liberal and Socialist governments have often resorted to this measure, and some employees, such as air traffic controllers, have operated under an emegency situation for weeks or months.

Public debate, mediation and arbitration

Law 1876 specifies the rights and obligations of employees before and during a strike. A recent amendment (law 1915, passed on 28 December 1990) stipulates as well that before a decision has been taken to strike, either employees or management may ask for a public discussion under the chairmanship of a mediator chosen through the procedures for mediation and arbitration specified by law 1876 (see below). The mediator must try to reach an agreement. If no agreement is reached within forty-eight hours, the mediator can publish alternative proposals in the daily press. Representatives of the press and other unions and employers' associations may be present at the discussion.

If agreement is reached, it has the force of a collective agreement. Failing an agreement, the parties may ask for mediation. If no settlement is reached within thirty days the mediator may make his or her own proposals: these will be deemed to have been rejected if neither party indicates acceptance within five days.

Law 1876 of 1990 specifies the right of unions, individual employers and employers' associations to ask for arbitration at any stage of the negotiations. If the unions ask for arbitration, they may not resort to a strike until ten days have elapsed from the application.

The arbitrator must make a decision within ten days if arbitration was preceded by mediation, or otherwise within 30 days. The decision takes the form and has the force of a collective agreement.

Law 1876 of 1990 established a Mediation and Arbitration Board. Its eleven-member board of directors consists of union, employer and state representatives, two university professors of labour economics and labour law respectively, and an independent person elected by the other board members on the basis of experience in industrial relations and their good standing.

Strikes

The right to strike is guaranteed by the constitution and statute law. Unions can take all necessary action within the framework of the law in order to promote the interests of workers and employees. Legal action and workers' interests are defined broadly. A strike can be decided by the most representative or by any other trade union.

Law 1915 of 1990, passed in the face of strong opposition from the unions, stipulates that employers have the right to dismiss:

- Employees on strike if the courts have declared the strike an abuse of power (by the unions) within twenty-four hours of a court ruling.
- Employees on lawful strike who prevent others going to work, occupy the premises or in any other way prevent the enterprise from functioning smoothly.
- Those who by law or collective agreements must work during a strike but do not follow management instructions.

Severance pay is obligatory for the employer in all such cases of dismissal (see the second volume in the European Management Guides series, *Terms and Conditions of Employment*).

In order to be lawful a strike must be carried on in pursuit of industrial demands (including trade union rights), and must be in solidarity with employees in another undertaking, or at the headquarters of a multinational company, provided the interests of the strikers are affected by the outcome of the action. Strike action requires a twenty-four-hour period of notice and must be preceded by a set of written demands, authorized by a recognized union and subject to a secret ballot. Other forms of industrial action are regarded as strikes and subject to the same legal requirements.

Both the 1982 and the 1990 legislation specify a number of essential services in which four days' notice must be given of industrial action, and a skeleton service must be maintained: such services include health, transport, sewage and refuse collection, civil aviation, the Bank of Greece, telecommunications, radio and television.

Lock-outs

Lock-outs are illegal under law 1264 of 1982. Employers can, however, take legal action if the law is broken by the strikers or by employees who, for safety or other reasons, must not participate in the strike.

Consequences of industrial action

Employees who are on strike cannot be sacked if the decision to strike was reached through legal procedures and the strikers have not broken the law. Even when the strike is over, sacking employees who took part in it could be judged by the courts an abuse of power.

Collective dismissal

Collective dismissals are regulated by law 1387 of 1983. It defines as a collective dismissal any dismissal on grounds not related to the employee in any undertaking employing more than twenty persons of:

- At least five employees in firms with twenty to fifty employees.
- Two to three per cent of the work force up to thirty employees in firms employing over fifty persons. (This percentage is reviewed and/or revised every six months by the Ministry, depending on labour market conditions.)

Employers must hold discussions with employee representatives, either trade unions or works councils, or if necessary a special committee if no other representation is available, on ways of minimizing the impact of redundancies, and must provide information on the grounds for the dismissals, the number of workers affected, their sex and occupation, and other relevant information. This information must also be forwarded to the local authorities, and to the local office of the labour administration, OAED.

The period of consultation with the work force can last up to twenty days. If the employer and work force agree, the dismissals will be deemed to have been approved, and may be effected ten days after the minutes of the consultations have been received by the authorities. Should no agreement be reached, the authorities can:

- Extend the consultation period by a further twenty days.
- Accept or reject the employer's proposal. Should the Ministry of Labour come to a decision, then the dismissals can proceed only within any limits laid down by the authorities. Any dismissals which exceed any such limits are null and void.

Severance payments are made in accordance with the rules for individual dismissals. For example, a white-collar employee with between four and six years' service would be entitled to three months' salary, halved if the required three months' written notice were given. (For severance payments for blue and white-collar workers, and periods of notice, see the second volume in the series of European Management Guides, *Terms and Conditions of Employment*, pp. 107–9.)

In 1988 effect was given to the EC directive on acquired rights via presidential decree 572/88.

Appendix

OAED (the state manpower and job placement agency:
Thrakis 8
166 10 Glyfada
Athens
tel. + 30 1 993 2589
fax + 30 1 993 7301

Ministry of Labour:
40 Piraeus Street
Athens
tel. + 30 1 523 2110

Federation of Greek Industries, SEB (represents employers in manufacturing and services, and negotiates general collective agreements with the Greek Confederation of Labour, the trade union centre):
5 Xenofontos Street
105 57 Athens
tel. + 30 1 323 7325

Greek Personnel Management
Association:
3 Karitsi Street
105 61 Athens
tel. + 30 1 322 5704

British–Hellenic Chamber of
Commerce:
25 Vas. Sofias
106 74 Athens
tel. + 30 1 721 0361
fax + 30 1 721 8571

GSEE (General Confederation of
Labour):
69, 28 October Street
Athens
tel. + 30 1 883 46 11
fax + 30 1 822 98 02

6

The Irish Republic

Industrial relations in Ireland are based on voluntarism, reflecting the common legal background shared with the British system, although basic trade union rights are constitutionally guaranteed. Recent legislation has created a more defined framework, but the law still generally serves to do no more than provide a context, together with machinery which the social partners can use for conciliation and arbitration. The Industrial Relations Act, 1990, replaces the former Trade Disputes Act, 1906, which had become divorced from practice and needs in many areas. The new legislation has caused controversy through the conditions which trade unions must meet to obtain a negotiating licence.

National structures of tripartite co-operation

In 1987 the main employer organization, the Federation of Irish Employers (FIE), the main trade union confederation, the Irish Congress of Trade Unions (ICTU) and the government agreed a three-year tripartite national agreement, the Programme for National Recovery (PNR). This agreement was the first of its kind and concentrated mainly on restricting basic pay increases to an annual 2·5 per cent as a key element in attempts to turn the economy round. The agreement also contained provisions on some aspects of terms and conditions, notably an employer commitment to negotiate a one-hour cut in the working week. The agreement was generally deemed to be successful. In early 1991 a further agreement, the Programme for Economic and Social Progress (PESP), was negotiated. This also limits pay increases over its three-year duration, but in addition gives scope for one locally bargained increase. These national tripartite agreements are not legally binding, but the compliance rate under the PNR was estimated at 95 per cent and current surveys show 80 per cent compliance with the PESP so far.

113

Advisory reports on various aspects of social and economic policy are drawn up by the National Economic and Social Council, which was set up by the government in 1973.

A bipartite body, the Employer–Labour Conference, was set up in the 1970s to help conclude a series of national pay understandings, and is made up of the FIE, representing private-sector employers, semi-state employer representatives, and the government as an employer, as well as representatives of the ICTU trade union confederation. It sets up working parties to monitor and research a variety of industrial relations subjects.

Employee participation

No statutory provision

There is no legislation governing employee participation in the private sector. In 1986 an Advisory Committee on Worker Participation reported on employee involvement and found no evidence of board-level participation in the private sector. However, at sub-board level a number of companies had developed a range of practices and procedures on a voluntary basis, each tailored to the individual needs of the company.

In June 1991 the ICTU and FIE issued a joint declaration on employee involvement in the private sector, prompted by a provision contained in the PESP tripartite national pact. The declaration supports moves towards employee involvement initiatives at local level in order to 'assist in the overall development of the enterprise, help to underpin the need to maximise competitiveness, encourage employees to identify with the objectives of the enterprise, and increase job satisfaction'. It recommends that the Irish Productivity Centre should be designated as the national organization to support attempts to develop company-level participation initiatives, by providing information, assistance and advice, and actively encouraging involvement. The declaration lists a variety of possible means of involvement for consideration by ICTU and FIE members, such as:

● General information-sharing by means of team briefings, 'open door' management, general meetings and attitude surveys.

- Consultation with employees and/or through representative mechanisms on issues including changes in work organization, training and skill development, equality and grading, recruitment and promotion, the state and performance of the company, and technological change.
- Task forces, involvement groups and quality circles.

The development of employee involvement throughout the private sector will be monitored by the Employer–Labour Conference. It is unlikely that there will be any legislation regulating employee participation in the private sector.

Although there is no statutory provision for formal employee consultation, consultation takes a variety of forms at company level. Independent studies have shown that over 50 per cent of employers in small companies consulted a trade union, although small companies tend to have a less well developed shop steward structure and less interaction with trade unions at official level than larger companies. Small firms do not use formal communication channels, although formal grievance and dispute procedures are more common. Larger companies will see good industrial relations practices as a priority, whereas much smaller companies, typically owner-managed, may tend to be unwilling to accept trade union structures at the workplace, favouring direct consultation with employees.

Legislation providing for employee representation does exist in the public sector. The Worker Participation (State Enterprises) Acts, 1977 and 1988, provide for the setting up of sub-board participative structures in thirty-five state enterprises. Around two-thirds of these enterprises have introduced employee participation arrangements. Their progress will be monitored under the PESP, as will the possibility of extending the provisions to more state enterprises. Some 269,000 people are employed in the public sector, accounting for 24 per cent of the work force.

At board level in the public sector, the legislation provides for elected worker representatives to fill up to a third of seats on the enterprise board. This number can vary as long as the number of worker representatives is not less than two. All full-time employees aged 18–65 with three years' service are eligible. Elections are held every four years.

Safety representatives

Under the Safety in Industry Act, 1980, employees have the right
to be represented by a safety representative in companies of up to
twenty employees, and a safety committee in larger companies. The
size of the committee varies according to the size of the company,
with one member for every twenty employees, up to a maximum of
ten members and with a minimum of three members. The employer
must consult the representative or committee on changes to the
working environment affecting the health or safety of employees,
and must consider any representations made by the committee or
representative concerning health and safety matters. Meetings of
the committee may take place in working time, with no loss of pay
for members, provided that meetings are not more frequent than
once every two months, do not last more than two hours and are
quorate.

Trade unions

Trade union structure

There is one main trade union confederation, the Irish Congress
of Trade Unions (ICTU), to which the majority of the sixty-odd
trade unions are affiliated. The ICTU has fifty-seven member
unions, covering 459,336 employees, according to ICTU data. It
is estimated that the ICTU accounts for around 93 per cent of total
union membership in the republic. Union density is around 50 per
cent, having risen quite sharply from 25 per cent in the post-war
period. Nevertheless, it has declined from a level of 55 per cent in
the late 1970s and is continuing to decline slightly, partly owing to
the growth of high-technology and service sectors, where there is
no strong tradition of unionization, and partly to the increase in
the number of temporary and casual workers.

There are a number of British-based trade unions in Ireland;
fifteen unions affiliated to the ICTU have their head offices in
Britain. However, these unions act virtually independently of their
UK head offices. Foreign-based unions do not have to register with
the Registrar of Friendly Societies in order to obtain a negotiation
licence (see below). However, a foreign-based union must be

recognized as a union under the law of the country in which its headquarters are situated.

The government has introduced a number of measures to help reduce the large number of unions. The Trade Union Act, 1975, was passed in order to facilitate mergers and currently offers financial aid to unions attempting to merge.

Unions are organized according to profession, or category of worker (e.g. white-collar), or are general unions, rather than being organized along political lines. Two large general unions account for around half the total ICTU-affiliated membership: SIPTU (Services Industrial Professional Technical Union), formed in 1990 through a merger between the unions ITGWU and FWUI, and by far the largest union with 197,000 members; and ATGWU (Amalgamated Transport and General Workers' Union), with 20,000 members. There are also a number of unions representing white-collar workers, the largest being the British-based MSF (Manufacturing Science Finance) with 20,721 members, and individual craft workers' unions such as the ETU (Electrical Trades Union). Separate unions cover the public service, and the fourteen public service unions affiliated to the ICTU account for 91,041 members. The largest public service union is IMPACT (Irish Municipal, Professional and Civil Trade Union), which was formed by a merger in early 1991 and has a total of 24,710 members.

The multiplicity of unions means that there is often more than one representative union in the workplace – one general union, one representing white-collar workers and one craft union. In general this does not cause industrial relations problems, as unions pursue single-table bargaining. In order to prevent inter-union disputes concerning membership, the ICTU's constitution contains rules governing the transfer of members between unions and settling disputes between unions.

Freedom of association

Under article 40 of the 1937 constitution every citizen, except certain categories of employee, such as members of the defence forces, has freedom of association and the right to form a trade union. This article has been interpreted in the courts to mean that the right to form a trade union also includes the right not to belong to a trade union. Consequently, it is deemed unconstitutional to take

industrial action to try to enforce a closed shop against the wishes
of other employees. Although there is freedom of association, trade
unions are not obliged to take every applicant into membership.

There is no positive right to strike but, as in the UK, trade
unions and their members enjoy a certain number of immunities
for acts in contemplation or furtherance of a trade dispute. These
immunities have been upheld in the Industrial Relations Act, 1990,
which replaced the Trade Disputes Act, 1906, the latter having been
entirely repealed. Immunities for individuals include organizing or
threatening to organize, or take part in, a strike, and taking part
in 'peaceful picketing'. Immunities do not exist for 'worker versus
worker' disputes, in cases concerning one worker only if agreed
procedures for the resolution of individual grievances have not
been exhausted, and in the case of industrial action taken contrary
to the outcome of a secret ballot (see below).

The regulation of trade unions

Under the Trade Union Act, 1871, a trade union is 'a combination,
whether temporary or permanent, for regulating the relations
between workmen and masters, or between workmen and workmen, or between masters and masters, or for imposing restrictive
conditions on the conduct of any trade or business as would have
been deemed to be an unlawful combination by reason of some
one or more of its purposes being in restraint of trade'. In order
to register as a trade union a union must apply to the Registrar of
Friendly Societies, who will subject its rules, objects and procedures
to inspection. If a registered union of employers or employees
wishes to bargain, it must obtain a negotiation licence from the
Ministry of Labour, issued only if the union can fulfil certain
conditions. Under the Trade Union Act, 1941, a minimum of seven
members was required for unions to apply for a negotiating licence.
Not surprisingly, this led to a proliferation of small unions. In order
to reverse the trend, the minimum membership requirement was
increased to 500 in 1971. The requirement was further increased
by the Industrial Relations Act, 1990, to 1,000. Other conditions
are as follows:

- Unions must make a deposit in the High Court, the amount
  varying according to size, ranging from Ir£20,000 for up to 2,000

members to Ir£60,000 for 35,000 and over.

- Union rule books must contain conditions of entry and cessation of membership and the register of members must be publicly accessible. Moreover, they must also contain a provision according to which the union will not engage in industrial action without a secret ballot (see below).
- Unions must notify the Labour Ministry and the ICTU eighteen months before applying for a licence, together with any trade union whose membership may overlap, and publish a notice in the daily newspapers.

The High Court may, at its discretion, waive the eighteen-month period of notice or the membership requirement, although in practice unions usually fulfil the membership requirement.

Recognition rights

There is no statutory obligation for an employer to recognize a trade union for bargaining purposes. However, in practice, employers usually recognize and negotiate with unions if they are representative of the employees or a particular section of employees within the company. In case law (*Becton Dickinson Ltd v. Lee*, 1973) a trade dispute concerning union recognition was held to be a valid dispute: 'if an employer refuses to treat with their [employees'] designated representative or spokesman, then that refusal can constitute a dispute which is connected with the employment or the terms of the employment of the workmen and, therefore, can be a trade dispute'.

Rights of trade union representatives

There is no statutory provision entitling trade union representatives to time off to carry out trade union activities. However, in practice, employers will allow trade union representatives to carry out their duties within working hours, especially if they are actively involved in bargaining, without loss of pay. The right to time off is sometimes enshrined in a house agreement. Some employers provide for union representatives to attend trade union education courses upon appointment.

Employers' organizations

Under Irish law, employers' organizations are governed by the same rules as trade unions. Under the Trade Union Act, 1941, they have to register as trade unions in order to gain a licence to engage in collective bargaining. The largest employer organization is the Federation of Irish Employers (FIE), a national body which has some 3,300 member companies. It offers a variety of advice and information services to members but does not negotiate industry agreements, although it does represent employers in tripartite talks at national level. There are also a number of industry-based employer organizations, the largest of which is the one representing construction employers, the Construction Industry Federation.

Bargaining

Although collective agreements are not statutorily defined as binding, case law generally deems collective agreements to be binding upon the signatory parties.

National-level

There is no legislation stipulating an obligation to bargain at any level. However, there was a series of national pay agreements throughout the 1970s, and the past three years have seen a national tripartite agreement on wage increases; a second three-year national agreement was negotiated at the beginning of 1991 following the expiry of the previous one. This national agreement is not legally binding but the compliance rate among companies tends to be high, at around 95 per cent for the previous national agreement.

Industry-level

Industry-level bargaining is not an important factor in the deter- .
mination of terms and conditions of employment and pay. However, there are some industry-level mechanisms which exist to set a floor for pay and terms and conditions. Joint labour

committees, which are set up and can be abolished by the Labour Court, exist in a number of sectors where there is low unionization. They consist of an equal number of employer and employee members, with an independent chair, and set minimum rates of pay and conditions in certain industries. Industries covered by such agreements include hairdressing, catering, hotels and some parts of the clothing industry. These minimum rates are set out in employment regulation orders, issued by the Ministry of Labour and binding on all employers in the industry. Failure to comply with an employment regulation order can incur a maximum fine of Ir£750, and employees can bring civil proceedings against employers through inspectors of the Department of Labour in order to enforce the order. Around 5 per cent of employees are covered by employment regulation orders.

Employers are liable to fines up to a maximum of Ir£500 for failing to comply with a requirement of a Department of Labour inspector in allowing access to premises or access to employment records.

The Labour Relations Commission, established by the Industrial Relations Act, 1990, in order to take over the advisory, arbitration and conciliation functions of the Labour Court, monitors the joint labour committees in order to determine whether new industries should be covered or old joint labour committees abolished. Applications for the creation of a new joint labour committee are made to the Labour Court, which will then reach a decision.

Joint Industrial Councils, independent bodies set up to promote harmonious industrial relations, may apply to the Labour Court for a Registered Employment Agreement containing pay and conditions provisions for sectors with a higher degree of unionization. Employers must keep records, for a period of three years, to show that the Registered Employment Agreement is being complied with, or be liable to a maximum fine of Ir£500. An employer who falsifies records is liable to a maximum fine of Ir£1,000 and/or imprisonment of up to three months.

Company-level

The bulk of collective bargaining is carried out at company level. There is no statutory obligation for employers to recognize, or bargain with, trade unions on matters relating to pay and working conditions. In practice, however, the rate of unionization among the work force is relatively high, and employers will bargain with union representatives if they are representative of the employees of the company. Bargaining usually takes place annually, with pay agreements concluded for the duration of one year. During the past three years most companies have allowed themselves to be bound by the national pay agreement. Recently some companies have concluded three-year agreements providing all the increases agreed in the current national agreement and have also negotiated a further increase of up to 3 per cent in accordance with the clause of the agreement allowing for one locally bargained increase. (For further information on pay determination, see the fourth volume in the European Management Guides series.)

Conciliation and arbitration

The Labour Relations Commission

The conciliation and arbitration system is totally voluntary. Official state conciliation and arbitration channels do exist but are there to provide the machinery with which the parties can solve a dispute rather than to back up legislation. Conciliation used to be provided by the Labour Court; however, under the Industrial Relations Act, 1990, a newly created body, the Labour Relations Commission, has taken over the conciliation services of the Labour Court, allowing the court to revert to a more judicial role and act as an institution of last resort. Cases can be referred to the Labour Court only after they have been through the conciliation procedures of the Labour Relations Commission. There are a few exceptions, such as:

- If the commission decides not to investigate the dispute, at the request of all the parties concerned.
- If the court decides that exceptional circumstances warrant its intervention without the dispute going through the commission.
- If the union, or both parties, indicate in advance that they will accept the recommendation of the court (section 20 of the Industrial Relations Act, 1969).
- If a recommendation has been issued by a Rights Commissioner or an Equality Officer, an appeal may go straight to the court.
- If the Minister of Labour believes that a dispute 'affects

the public interest' he or she may refer it straight to the court.

Under the Industrial Relations Act, 1990, the Labour Relations Commission may draw up codes of practice on industrial relations issues in consultation with trade unions, employers' organizations and other interested parties on its own initiative or at the request of the Minister of Labour. These codes are not legally binding, although if an employer is found to have been flouting them it will be taken into consideration in the case of a dispute. The commission is currently drafting its first code of practice, which will relate to strikes in essential services, following a strike at the state electricity company, ESB, in the spring of 1991.

If disputes cannot be settled at company level (although a vast majority are), the matter can be taken to an industrial relations officer from the conciliation service of the Labour Relations Commission. If the dispute is still unresolved, i.e. the parties do not accept the recommendation made by the industrial relations officer, the matter can be taken to the Labour Court, whose decision is final but not enforceable.

Rights Commissioners

Rights Commissioners act under the jurisdiction of the Labour Relations Commission and are involved in individual disputes and those concerning a body of workers which are not connected with pay rates, working time or holidays. Hearings before a Rights Commissioner are informal and the recommendation is not binding. If either of the parties wishes to appeal against the recommendation to the Labour Court, the court must be notified in writing within six weeks of the recommendation.

Disputes relating to the Redundancy Payments Acts, 1967–84, the Minimum Notice and Terms of Employment Acts, 1973–84, the Unfair Dismissals Act, 1977, and the Maternity Protection of Employees Act, 1981, can be heard before an Employment Appeals Tribunal. Its decision is binding on matters relating to the Redundancy or Minimum Notice Acts; parties may appeal to the circuit court against recommendations made concerning the Unfair Dismissal Act and the Maternity Protection of Employees Act.

Industrial action

The right to strike

There is no positive right to strike in Irish law. The Industrial
Relations Act, 1990, maintains the principle of immunity for
individuals and trade unions for certain acts 'done in contemplation
or furtherance of a trade dispute' which would normally be
unlawful. However, immunity applies only if a number of conditions
are met:

- The action must not have been rejected in a ballot.
- The action taken must be of a kind permitted by legislation and
  should be a trade dispute as defined by legislation.
- All agreed procedures for conciliation must have been used if
  the dispute concerns an individual worker.

Permitted industrial action

A trade dispute is defined under the 1990 Act as 'any dispute
between employers and workers which is connected with the
employment or non-employment, or the terms or conditions of
or affecting the employment of, any person'. Therefore, disputes
between employees are not seen as official trade disputes. There
are a number of subjects which are seen by the Act as not forming
a valid basis for industrial action, such as:

- Any dispute aimed at trying to enforce a closed shop.
- Any dispute concerned with a purely political issue.
- Disputes concerning the commercial interests of the employer
  which do not affect the work force in any way.

Ballots

At present there is no statutory obligation upon unions to hold a
ballot before strike action is taken. However, under the Industrial
Relations Act, 1990, within two years from the enactment of the
legislation (18 July 1990) all trade unions registered or operating in
Ireland must include a clause in their rule book providing for a secret
ballot of the members concerned before engaging in strike action:

'the committee of management or other controlling authority of a trade union shall not organise, participate in, sanction or support a strike or other industrial action against the wishes of a majority of its members voting in a secret ballot, except where, in the case of ballots by more than one trade union, an aggregate majority of all the votes cast favours such strike or other industrial action'. If this provision is not included in union rule books within two years the Registrar of Friendly Societies will instruct the union to comply with the requirement and may revoke the union's negotiating licence if the union does not comply. In practice the majority of unions already provide for ballots in their rule books.

Injunctions

The 1990 Act has made a number of changes in the law on injunctions. Previously, employers could take out interim *ex parte* injunctions in order to stop strike action. Under the new legislation, provided the industrial action has been approved by secret ballot and the appropriate notice has been given, employers cannot obtain an *ex parte* injunction. If the employer gives notice of intention to apply for an injunction, it will be heard in court, but an injunction will not be granted if the union can prove that the action is in contemplation or furtherance of a trade dispute as defined by law. These new provisions mean that employers will probably find it more difficult to obtain injunctions than was previously the case.

Lock-outs

The Unfair Dismissals Act, 1977, defines a lock-out as 'an action which, in contemplation or furtherance of a trade dispute . . . is taken by one or more employers, whether parties to the dispute or not, and which consists of the exclusion of one or more employees from one or more factories, offices or other places of work or of the suspension of work in one or more such places or of the collective, simultaneous or otherwise connected termination or suspension or employment of a group of employees'.

The Act states that dismissals are deemed to be unfair if employees are locked out and not re-engaged or reinstated when work is resumed. Lock-outs may therefore be regarded as legal if all employees are reinstated.

Picketing

Under the Industrial Relations Act, 1990, employees may engage in primary picketing provided that the picket is peaceful, that it takes place at the employer's place of business, that the picketers are employed by the employer in dispute and that the action is taken 'in contemplation or furtherance of a trade dispute'. Trade union officials may accompany their members on the picket line. ICTU may grant an 'all-out picket' to unions in a dispute, in which a total withdrawal of all trade union members in an employment is sought and not merely those directly in dispute with the employer, provided that all union members vote in a secret ballot and the aggregate of the votes support the proposal.

No distinction was drawn between primary and secondary picketing under the Trade Disputes Act, 1906. However, the 1990 Act states that secondary picketing is permitted if it is 'reasonable for those who are so attending to believe . . . that the employer has directly assisted their employer who is a party to the trade dispute for the purpose of frustrating the strike'. Even though there is now a clear definition of secondary picketing under the new law it will still be difficult to establish that an employer was deliberately assisting an employer in dispute with a view to frustrating a strike. Employers in the health service which maintain life-preserving services may not be subjected to secondary picketing.

Contracts of employment

According to case law based on the Minimum Notice and Terms of Employment Act, 1973, the contract of employment of a striking employee will be held to be suspended, not breached, if they give one week's notice to the employer before taking strike action. Collective agreements or individual contracts may require longer periods of notice.

Contracts are suspended for the duration of the strike. If employees are sacked whilst on strike they can claim unfair dismissal under the Unfair Dismissals Act, 1977, if other employees taking part in the strike action were not dismissed or if other employees were subsequently reinstated or re-engaged and the persons in question were not.

Employees on strike do not receive pay from the employer for the duration of the strike. Unions do grant strike pay but it varies according to the financial situation of the union and the number of employees on strike. Employees on strike may not claim unemployment benefit but if the striker has adult and child dependants they may claim supplementary welfare allowances. Strikers may also claim a tax rebate for the period during which they were not receiving a regular salary.

Collective dismissal

Statutory provisions

Under the Protection of Employment Act, 1977, passed in order to bring Irish law into line with the EC directive on collective dismissals, employers in firms with twenty or more employees must consult work-force representatives and the Ministry of Labour thirty days before effecting a collective dismissal. A collective dismissal is defined as dismissal within thirty days of:

- At least five employees in companies of twenty-one to forty-nine employees.
- At least ten employees in companies of fifty to ninety-nine employees.
- At least 10 per cent of employees in companies of 100–299 employees.
- At least thirty employees in companies of 300 or more employees.

When notifying the Ministry of Labour the employer must include details concerning:

- The company and the establishment effecting the redundancies.
- The number of employees in the company.
- Details of the employees to be made redundant, the proposed date of the redundancies and the reasons for them.
- Details of employee representatives and the consultations which have taken place with those representatives.

A copy of this information should also be sent to employee representatives.

Employee representatives should be consulted on:

- The reasons for the redundancies.
- The number of employees to be made redundant, and the date of the redundancies.
- The criteria used in the selection of employees for redundancy.
- Ways in which to avoid or reduce the impact of the redundancies.

Employers must keep all records of collective dismissals for a period of three years.

If employers carry out a collective dismissal before the thirty-day period expires they are liable to a fine of up to Ir£3,000, and of up to Ir£500 for failing to keep records of the dismissals. The fines may be waived if employers can prove that they did not hold consultations or make the redundancies within the thirty-day period because business reasons made compliance with the Act impossible.

Employers must inform the employees concerned of the proposed redundancies; periods of notice vary according to length of service, ranging from one week to eight weeks.

Severance pay

Full-time employees with at least two years' service who are made redundant are entitled to service-related severance payments amounting to half a week's pay for each year of service between the ages of 16 and 41, plus one week's pay for each year of service over the age of 41, plus the equivalent of one week's pay. This covers weekly earnings up to a ceiling of Ir£250. These payments are lump sums; employers can usually claim 60 per cent of statutory severance payments from the Redundancy Fund, which is financed by employer contributions of 0·05 per cent of earnings up to a ceiling of Ir£13,000 per annum.

In practice it is not unusual for unions to negotiate higher severance payments with employers. Payments may range from the statutory minimum only to six weeks' pay per year of service in addition to the statutory minimum.

Transfer of undertakings

Under the European Communities (Safeguarding of Employees' Rights on Transfer of Undertakings) Regulations, 1980, employee representatives must be informed and consulted, by both the original and the future employers, in the case of any transfers of business. Information, given 'in good time', must contain details such as the reasons for the transfer of business, the implications of the move for the employees and any changes which may affect the employees. If no employee representatives exist, all employees must be informed individually in a written letter and the information must also be posted up at the workplace.

Employee rights are protected upon the transfer of a business or part of a business to other employers following a transfer or merger. The rights and obligations of the original employer with regard to employment contracts are transferred to the new employer. The terms and conditions of any collective agreement must be respected until its date of expiry unless it is replaced by a new agreement.

Employees cannot be dismissed on the sole grounds of the transfer of a business. However, they can be dismissed for economic reasons or structural changes in the work force.

Appendix

Department of Labour:
Mespil Road
Dublin 4
tel. (01) 765861

Federation of Irish Employers
(FIE):
Baggot Bridge House
84–6 Lower Baggot Street
Dublin 2
tel. (01) 601011
fax (01) 601717

Irish Congress of Trade Unions
(ICTU):
19 Raglan Road
Dublin 4
tel. (01) 680641
fax (01) 609027

Institute of Personnel
Management:
35–9 Shelbourne Road
Ballsbridge
Dublin 4
tel. (01) 686244

Labour Court:
Tom Johnson House
Haddington Road
Dublin 4
tel. (01) 608444

Labour Relations Commission:
Haddington Road
Dublin 4
tel. (01) 608444

Employer–Labour Conference:
Davitt House
Mespil Road
Dublin 4
tel. (01) 681324

Employment Appeals Tribunal:
Davitt House
Mespil Road
Dublin 4
tel. (01) 765861

Irish Productivity Centre:
IPC House
35–9 Shelbourne Road
Dublin 4
tel. (01) 686244

7

Italy

Italian industrial relations are characterized by a coherent structure based on an established pattern of collective agreements covering areas often typically regulated by statute in other European Community countries. The law, principally the 1970 Workers' Statute, essentially provides a framework of protective rights, leaving employers and employees discretion on how to structure themselves and their relationship to one another. Employers' associations and trade unions are *de facto* organizations and have no legal personality. Under the law, employers and employees are not obliged to negotiate, nor to sign contracts. The freedom to enter into contracts (*libertà di contrattazione*) implies complete freedom in the choice of mechanisms for the conclusion of any agreements considered necessary. Information disclosure is regulated by collective agreement.

Compared with the 1970s, industrial relations in the private sector have been markedly less conflictual, although the public sector has frequently found itself the subject of disruptive action by unofficial union organizations, culminating in legislation being passed to curb industrial action in the public sector.

National structures

There is no formal institutional mechanism for tripartite bargaining, but there is extensive tripartite discussion on fundamental issues; in the past these have covered such matters as reform of the *scala mobile* pay indexation system, and in 1991 there has been a focus on Italy's international competitiveness, and specifically on employers' social charges, on taxation and on bargaining arrangements in the public sector.

There is a well established practice of bipartite bargaining at national level between employers' confederations such as Confindustria and the three trade union centres CGIL, CISL

131

and UIL (see below). Occasionally the government will become involved in negotiations where issues of concern to all employees are involved and the partners are looking for external mediation.

Agreements reached at this level often effectively replace legislation, and can eventually become law. For example, procedures on collective dismissal were regulated by a national agreement, widely adhered to even by non-signatories, until legislation was passed in 1991 (see below). Moreover, collective bargaining at national level also often takes on the role of fleshing out and implementing statute law (so-called 'bargained laws'), as has happened on atypical employment. During 1990–91 talks have been in progress on basic reforms of industrial relations. Particular attention has been devoted to formalizing bargaining arrangements, and specifically which levels of bargaining should regulate which matters, and which should be most influential in setting pay and conditions. Whilst Confindustria has been seeking greater decentralization, the trade unions have been seeking to retain a prominent role for industry-level bargaining.

In practice, both tripartite and bipartite talks often become intertwined, with compromises in one set made conditional on – typically – government action in another. In addition, simultaneous sets of bilateral discussions may also take place, with each of the three partners meeting one of the others in a cycle of meetings.

The National Economic and Employment Council (*Consiglio Nazionale dell' Economia e del Lavoro*, CNEL) is a tripartite body established in 1947 whose responsibilities include giving opinions on legislation, preparing its own proposals and suggesting draft legislation, and undertaking surveys. It has also been given the task of maintaining a data base of collective agreements.

Workplace employee representation

There are no statutory mechanisms for employee participation in the form encountered in countries such as Germany, France or the Netherlands. Rather, the 1970 Workers' Statute offers a framework of protective rights for trade union organization, which effectively ratified forms of representation forged during the 1969 'hot autumn' of industrial conflict. Institutions for employee representation at the workplace are a product of these trade union rights, rather than independent forms.

Rights under collective agreements

Employees have information rights under industry agreements rather than under the law. The metalworking agreement, for example, makes the following provisions, based on a recognition of managerial prerogatives. Rights are granted both at different levels (central, region, company) as well as on specific subjects.

At *central* level, a data bank was to be established to monitor new technology, employment trends particularly where new equipment has been introduced, changes in female employment, especially in the south, investment trends in the industry, labour costs compared with other OECD countries, changes in hours actually worked.

At *regional* level, local employer associations will give broad information to regional trade union organizations on the production prospects of the industry in the region, employment trends, with special attention to industrial restructuring (which may lead to negotiations on job losses and redundancy arrangements; see below), the establishment and location of new plants, female employment trends, home working and training for middle managers and specialists.

At *company* level, in firms with more than 200 employees the employer must provide information to works councils (see below) on any significant change to the production process and the technology being used, on changes in the overall organization of work which might impinge on employment levels, decentralization of production, and large-scale permanent transfers of employees. Where there are more than 350 employees, information must be provided on investment and the employment and environmental impact of new operations or an extension of existing operations.

Workplace representation

Employee representation at the workplace is established on the basis of the right guaranteed to trade unions to set up representative organizations at workplace level under the 1970 Workers' Statute. However, the initiative in setting up workplace institutions must

Proposals for change

In spring 1991 proposals were agreed between the main union centres to replace the works councils, generically called *rappresentanze sindacali aziendali* (RSA), by a so-called 'unitary union representative' body, *rappresentanze sindacali unitarie* or RSU. The changes to electoral procedures contained in the agreement aim to tackle the problems of union discipline and declining membership. In recent years the old structure has been viewed increasingly as unrepresentative because of changes in the profile of the work force, in technology and in the economic circumstances of private-sector companies. Though the details have yet to be finalized, the framework of the agreement is in place. Unitary trade union representatives will be elected at the workplace (or at territorial level in small firms) by all employees, including non-unionists, for a two-year period of office. (In some workplaces the same people have sat on the works council for up to ten years without re-election.) Candidates standing for election must either be members of the three main official unions or must have the support of at least 5 per cent of all workers eligible to vote. Elections are valid only if there is at least a 51 per cent turn-out.

Company agreements made by workplace representatives are valid for the whole of the company work force, whether they are members of a trade union or not. Problems arise when a group of workers call into question the representativeness of the works council and hence effectively challenge the validity of the agreement. The new machinery aims to promote a common front on the union side, and the new framework agreement specifically states this intention as well as outlining procedures for cases where the unions do not agree among themselves. At the time of going to press this machinery has yet to be approved by the employers' confederations.

Trade unions

Trade union and employer freedom of association is enshrined in the 1970 Workers' Statute, which not only makes clear what the freedom is but also outlines a series of sanctions should it be encroached upon. The Workers' Statute guarantees the following rights:

address the issue more fundamentally by reorganizing their structures.

Rights of trade union representatives

Apart from the right to represent members at the workplace and to be involved in bargaining, members of works councils (*dirigenti sindacali*) may not be dismissed, except for serious misconduct, and may not be transferred without the prior consent of the works council. In addition they are entitled to certain time-off rights. The entitlement is usually at least eight hours per month.

For each union the following number of delegates are entitled to leave of absence:

* One delegate in companies employing fewer than 200 employees in the category for which the union branch was established.
* One delegate for every 300 employees (or fraction of that number) in companies employing up to 3,000 employees in the category for which the union branch was established.
* In larger workplaces, one delegate for every 500 employees (or fraction of that number) in the category for which the union branch was established, in addition to the minimum of one delegate per 300 employees.

The statute states that union officials are also entitled to unpaid leave of up to eight days a year to pursue union activities. Collective agreements may improve on the law's provisions and identify particular categories of employee representative (*dirigente sindacale*) falling within the scope of special protection or enjoying particular rights.

Employees elected to trade union office at national or provincial level are entitled, under clause 31 of the Workers' Statute, to unpaid leave of absence at their request at any time during, or for the entire duration of, their term of office.

Trade union structure

There are three major trade union confederations, organized, broadly speaking, along political lines: the CGIL is oriented towards the Communist Party, now reconstituted as the Party of the Democratic Left (PDS); the CISL towards the Christian Democrats; and the UIL towards the Socialists. In July 1972 the three confederations came together in a 'United Federation' (*Federazione Unitaria*) which guaranteed each confederation's identity and independence but, at the same time, built a common structure for collective bargaining with employers and for negotiation with government, within a broad reference framework for united trade union action. In the spring of 1984, however, the Federazione Unitaria broke up following disagreements between the union confederations over a decree introduced on 14 February 1984 to reform the *scala mobile* system of wage indexation and reduce its impact on labour costs. While the CISL and the UIL broadly supported the decree, the pro-communist CGIL withdrew its support at the last minute, bringing to an end the united trade union front.

Each of these confederations has affiliated unions organized by industry or sector – engineering, textiles, banking, and so on. Workers are therefore organized vertically by political allegiance, as well as horizontally by sector. In engineering, for example, workers belong to the CGIL-affiliated Fiom, to the CISL-affiliated Fim, or to the Uilm, whose members are affiliated to the UIL. These sector-level federations (*federazioni unitarie di categoria*) were further united in the Federation of Metalworkers (*Federazione Lavoratori Metalmeccanici*) from 1972, although inter-confederal co-operation within this particular industry federation was seriously weakened by differences over the reform of the *scala mobile* in the mid-1980s. Similar national federations were formed for other sectors (Fulta in textiles, Fulc in chemicals, Fib in banking, and so on). Some of these sector-level federations have remained active despite the break-up of the Federazione Unitaria at national level.

In 1989 about 40 per cent of Italian employees were organized in the three main trade union confederations. However, much of the apparent ability of the unions to sustain their membership is attributable to the inclusion of non-active retired members. This effect has been reinforced by the operation of the unique Italian redundancy system, which has kept workers on within their previous industries who would have been dismissed in other countries (see below). Outside the official structure there are also unofficial or 'autonomous' unions (the 'Cobas' or grass-roots committees), principally in the public sector – the health service, transport, and so on. Such organizations are usually concerned principally with the maintenance of differentials for higher-paid groups of workers and have been seen as a product of the tendency for differentials to be eroded through national industry pay agreements. The main trade union confederations are set out below.

The CGIL, which claimed about 5 million members in 1990, is the largest of the three main union confederations. It is oriented towards the Communist Party, now the PDS, though a significant minority of its membership is Socialist – by tradition the deputy General Secretary is always a Socialist. The CGIL's influence is centred principally in engineering and heavy industry.

The CISL, with 3·5 million members in 1990 (1·2 million of them pensioners), has close links with the Christian Democrat Party and broke away from the CGIL in 1948.

The UIL has close links with the Socialist Party. It had approximately 1,560,000 members in 1990 and tends to recruit from the higher grades in industry. It left the CGIL in 1950.

The FNDAI is the largest association negotiating on behalf of Italy's estimated 90,000 industrial managers. It claims a membership of around 50,000, represents industrial managers across all sectors, and negotiates with employers' organizations in both the private and the public sector.

The FNDAC negotiates on behalf of 18,426 (1990) commercial managers, of whom 2,388 are pensioners.

Organizations representing senior white-collar staff (*quadri*)

Senior white-collar staff with technical and managerial responsibilities were for a long time unrecognized as a separate category of employee under Italian law. However, after much parliamentary lobbying, legal recognition was finally granted through an amendment to article 2095 of the Civil Code, passed by the Senate on 23 April 1985. Under the amendment employers are required to establish, through collective bargaining, which of their employees come into this category. The process was to take place within one year of the amendment's appearance in the official gazette. Although Italy's 700,000 or so *quadri* have now been given legal recognition the national organizations which represent many of them have still not been given legal bargaining rights. These organizations do, however, act as pressure groups and have some influence on the bargaining practices of the unions.

Employers' organizations

These are organized according to economic sector – industry, commerce, agriculture, crafts – according to whether they are in the public sector and often according to size. They are not regulated by statutory provisions.

Confindustria, established in 1910, is the largest employers' organization in the private sector and in the early 1980s embraced more than 100,000 companies employing about 3 million people. As well as co-ordinating employers' action at local and regional level, Confindustria represents private-sector industry in national talks with the unions and with government, and signs national-level agreements with the main trade union confederations. It has a special internal body representing the interests of smaller companies. It is divided regionally and provincially into smaller units, such as Assolombarda (the largest of the regional bodies). In addition, it counts among its members over 100 national professional or national industry federations such as Federmeccanica (see below), Federchimica and Federtessile.

Intersind is the employers' organization representing publicly owned companies in the engineering industry. It was set up in 1958 following a government directive providing for separate employer representation in the public and private sectors. ASAP represents employers in publicly owned companies in the petrochemical industry. Federmeccanica represents employers in the private sector of the engineering industry. It is the largest employers' federation belonging to Confindustria, and represents over 10,000 companies employing around 1·2 million people. Confapi represents small and medium-size companies in the private sector (although Confindustria also does so). It was set up following the creation during the 1950s of a provincial organization representing small employers.

Levels of bargaining

Agreements between employers and unions may take place at three levels:

- National.
- Industry/sector.
- Company/plant.

There are no rules governing what may be bargained within each level.

National level

National agreements are occasionally negotiated between Confindustria and union confederations. Examples include the agreement of 25 January 1975 which reformed the wage indexation system (*scala mobile*) and the agreement of 26 January 1977 on labour costs and productivity (both of which have been overtaken by subsequent events). Negotiations are taking place between Confindustria and the union confederations with a view to changing the institutional framework for conducting industrial relations. Very occasionally, also, agreements are negotiated between Confindustria, union confederations and government. Such tripartite agreements are rare, however. By far the most significant in recent years was the tripartite central agreement on labour costs (the Scotti agreement) signed on 22 January 1983.

Industry/sector level

Sector-level bargaining is important, as it is the level at which minimum wage rates are established for each industry. (There is no national minimum wage.)

For each sector – such as engineering, construction, textiles, and so on – there are usually three sectoral agreements. These cover:

- The private sector.
- Publicly owned companies (*a partecipazione statale*).
- The small business or craft sector (*artigianato*).

There is sometimes more than one agreement in the small business sector. With around twenty-five major industries in the economy there are a total of 100 or so national industry agreements.

There is no regional or provincial bargaining, and the regional bargaining area (*gabbia salariale*) was abolished in 1966 except in agriculture, where regional differences in rates are still permitted. Regional differences may, however, be established through company or plant-level agreements.

Company/plant level

In the year following the conclusion of a national-level agreement, unions usually negotiate at company or plant level for improvements on the minima laid down at industry level. These improvements (*superminimi*) then form the basic rate from which bonuses, overtime rates and so on are calculated. Hundreds of such company-level agreements are in existence.

Collective agreements at company or plant level are between employee representatives (*rappresentanze sindacali aziendali*, RSA) and the company or plant management. As well as supplementary company pay, they cover issues such as the organization of work and working time, the insertion of workers into the grading structure, health and safety, production bonuses, and information on company plans affecting investment and employment. Company or plant agreements generally seek to improve upon terms and conditions laid down in national industry agreements or at the very least to ensure that the basic terms and conditions set down at industry level are correctly implemented. They also seek to work out specific applications of any general provisions laid down by national industry agreements (such as flexible working time arrangements). However, in law there is no hierarchy of agreements, and company agreements could theoretically introduce a worsening of terms and conditions as well an improvement, provided it did not break the law. Often issues to be covered in company agreements are laid down in national industry agreements.

The pay bargaining system, therefore, is based on a network of national agreements fixing minimum rates, plus company and plant agreements which improve on these minima to varying degrees. The difference between minimum and actual rates varies considerably, according to the industry, the type of company and even the region: large factories in the north may pay up to 30 per cent above the minimum national rates as a result of local bargaining.

Validity and duration of agreements

Validity of agreements

National industry agreements are binding on all employers in a sector, irrespective of whether they are members of a signatory organization. Two mechanisms ensure this. First, should a non-signatory employer implement one term of an agreement in their industry, they are deemed to have accepted all its terms. Second, the social security organization INPS requires employers to indicate the collective agreement to which employees are subject when making returns for compulsory social insurance contributions. Section 46 of the constitution also provides that 'The worker has the right to a payment which is proportional to the quantity and quality of his work and which in any case is sufficient to ensure for himself and his family a free and dignified existence,' 'The maximum working day is established by law' and 'The worker has the right to a weekly rest and paid annual holidays and cannot renounce them.'

The civil courts (*preture*), which have developed functions as labour tribunals, have interpreted the phrase 'payment . . . to ensure . . . a free and dignified existence' as the basic rate established by collective agreement in the relevant industry. In this the civil courts have always been supported in the appeal courts (*cassazione*). Thus employers are obliged to pay the basic rate even if they themselves are not party to the agreement. The courts have interpreted the 'basic rate' to include 'thirteenth month' payments, which are now virtually universal, but not fourteenth, fifteenth or sixteenth month payments.

In contrast, civil servants' and other public employees' organizations bargain with the government and local authorities. Agreements must be ratified by Parliament or the local council before they acquire the force of law.

There is, therefore, no single minimum rate of pay for the whole country, but rather a series of minima for different industries. These minima are revised each time an industry agreement is renegotiated. Because of the '*scala mobile*' pay indexation system, however, these account for a relatively small proportion of the total pay packet.

Workers then bargain at plant or company level for improvements on the basic agreements which equally have the force of law once negotiated.

Duration of agreements

The duration of a collective agreement is set out in its provisions. Most industry agreements last for three years and form the framework of plant or company-level negotiations in the year following conclusion.

Monitoring of agreements

Minimum rates are subject to monitoring both by the local labour inspectorate, whose officials have the right to examine a company's books, and the trade unions, whose representatives will rapidly take up grievances.

An employer paying less than the agreed minimum rate may be sued by an employee and fined. No formal notification of change in minimum rates is given to the individual employer. Since the minima are legally enforceable, employers are expected to be aware of them. However, employers' organizations may always be consulted in cases of doubt.

Conciliation and arbitration

Conciliation and arbitration are not widespread, and in all cases consist of a voluntary procedure laid down – if at all – by collective agreement. Conciliation may normally take one of two forms:

- In civil courts (*conciliazione giudiziaria*), once a problem has arisen.
- Through the provincial conciliation commissions (*commissioni provinciali di conciliazione*), which were set up under law 533 of 11 August 1973.

These commissions are based at the headquarters of each provincial labour office (*sede provinciale dell'Ufficio del Lavoro*). They are chaired by the labour office, presiding over a panel of employers' and union representatives. Sub-committees may also be set up as appropriate.

Arbitration may, under article 4 of law 533 of 1973, be undertaken only if explicitly referred to in a collective agreement and is an uncommon procedure.

Industrial action

No formal procedures exist for handling the breakdown of talks. *In extremis*, where an important national industry agreement is being negotiated, the Minister of Labour will step in and mediate. With the exception of what is laid down in self-regulatory codes and in law 146 of 1990 (see below) on strikes in essential public services, employees do not have to give notice of their intention to take industrial action unless the safety of persons or plant is endangered. In that case the length of notice should be sufficient to allow for the setting up of adequate safety measures.

Ballots are not required before strike action is taken. Italian law grants all employees a positive right to strike, with any kind of industrial action permitted. Even political strikes are legal, provided they do not aim to overthrow the constitution.

Strike action in essential services

In June 1990 the government introduced a new law to regulate strike action in essential services, overwhelmingly provided by the public sector. Provision for such a law had always existed under the constitution but had never previously been enacted. However, frequent disruption of public services and the reaction of public opinion finally forced the government's hand. For many, however, the new law does not go far enough and they claim it has no teeth. Law 146 provides:

- A non-exhaustive list of essential services (those deemed necessary 'to guarantee basic human rights to life, health, liberty, security, welfare, education and freedom of communication'), where the right to strike is limited to guarantee users a minimum level of service.
- Regulations governing *la precettazione* – a legal notice served

on individual workers requiring them to present themselves for work – in existence since the 1930s.

- The formation of a commission to ensure proper implementation of the law.

The minimum level of service is defined by national industry collective agreements, which must identify essential services in their sectors both in the public and in the private sector. Disputes are referred to, and on request arbitrated by, the commission, which consists of nine members appointed by both Houses of Parliament. Workers are required to give employers ten days' notice of strike action and of its duration, and organizations affected must give the public five days' notice. To ensure a minimum level of service, workers may be ordered to present themselves for work. Failure to comply with such an order incurs a fine: the order can be challenged in a court of law within seven days of its receipt.

Infringement of the law will attract sanctions, which can apply to individuals (but exclude dismissal) as well as to organizations. They include fines, withdrawal of paid leave and suspension.

Union codes of conduct

To avoid legal intervention on the right to strike, the three main trade union centres, the CGIL, CISL and UIL, had drawn up voluntary codes of conduct to be followed prior to strike action. The codes, however, applied only to their members and were not respected by independent organizations, in particular the Cobas. For this reason the traditional unions gave their support to law 146 of 1990, particularly as it refers the minimum level of service to be provided to the collective bargaining process.

Employers' industrial action

As with employees, so the law permits employers to undertake industrial action in the form of a lock-out, provided it is not in response to trade union strike action. In such a case a lock-out would be considered anti-union behaviour, under article 28 of the Workers' Charter.

Conduct during industrial action

Peaceful picketing is legal provided no acts of violence are committed to workers wishing to work and no damage is done to the plant. If either should occur, then the individuals concerned would be held liable.

Consequences of lawful industrial action

During strike action an employee's contract of employment is deemed suspended and therefore employees are not entitled to payment for the period during which the strike takes place.

However, the employer must pay all social contributions as usual, and periods of strike action do not affect length of service payments. Workers who take strike action are protected from dismissal or disciplinary action under sections 15, 16 and 28 of the Workers' Statute. Under the law sacked workers can be reinstated and/or the employer fined.

Consequences of unlawful strike action

Strike action is unlawful only if it infringes the provisions of law 146 of 1990 regulating strike action in essential public services. In such a case individuals or organizations can be sanctioned according to the severity of the violation; measures which terminate or alter the employment relationship, however, are excluded. Sanctions can include fines, withdrawal of paid leave or suspension.

Settling disputes

There are no formal procedures for settling disputes. Disputes are settled mainly by strike action followed by collective bargaining. In serious cases government ministers will mediate.

Collective dismissal

Legislation passed in July 1991 finally enacted EC directive 75/129 on collective dismissals. Under the new law collective dismissals are defined as those which because of a reduction in or change of activity affect five or more employees in a particular unit of production within a time span of 120 days. 'Mobility' (redundancy) procedures and criteria will apply (see below). Dismissed workers with at least twelve months' service and employed on a full-time contract will be entitled to 'mobility' (redundancy) payments. Should such workers be subsequently reinstated, the company is entitled to lay off an equal number of workers in their place without having to start a new procedure, provided the correct criteria are used and the workers' representatives are informed.

Redundancy procedure

Though the new legislation introduces redundancy procedures they are acted upon only as a last resort when companies have exhausted their entitlement to the lay-off fund, the special *cassa integrazione* fund (*cassa integrazione straordinaria*, see below). If reinstatement is not possible at this point, they may institute redundancy procedures. To do so they must inform the workers' representative body and the appropriate industry union, which, with the company, will jointly examine:

• Why the need to reduce personnel has arisen.
• The possibility of using the excess labour in a different way and/or flexible working time.

If no agreement is arrived at, the provincial labour authority will attempt conciliation. When an agreement is reached or the procedure is exhausted the company may move to terminate the employees' employment, although such workers enjoy a special status ('mobility') in terms of subsequent job search through the state placement system and receive continuing payments in addition to the statutory severance payment (*trattamento di fine rapporto* – see the second volume of the European Management Guides). The end of the employment contract must be communicated in writing to individual workers, who must be given the appropriate period of notice. Workers made redundant are entitled to payments lasting between twelve and thirty-six months, depending on age. In any event, payment must not be made for a period longer than the person's period of service.

Redundant workers are also entitled to priority when the company undertakes new recruitment. They can be recruited on temporary contracts not exceeding one year's duration, with the added incentive of reduced rates of employer social contributions. These reduced rates can last for one year even if the temporary contract becomes a permanent one. In cases where workers are reinstated on full-time contracts, the employer is entitled to draw 50 per cent of any redundancy pay to which the workers would still have been entitled.

Criteria for choosing redundant workers

Workers can be made redundant only for technical, production or organizational reasons and according to criteria laid down by collective agreement. Where no agreement exists the following (unfortunately competing) criteria must be used:

- Number of dependants.
- Length of service.
- Technical, productive and organizational demands.

Termination of contract is null and void if the correct procedures and criteria are not used, and the employees affected will be entitled to reinstatement.

Temporary or partial unemployment: the *cassa integrazione*

As noted, collective dismissals are carried out only as a last resort. Prior to these Italy still retains its unique system of dealing with those laid off or put on to short-term working for economic reasons or by virtue of restructuring. This lay-off fund (*cassa per l'integrazione dei guadagni*, or CIG for short) has been extensively used and abused in situations where, in other countries, workers would have been dismissed. The CIG is funded by employer contributions but payments from it have had to be considerably boosted by state aid to maintain its solvency. Payments from the fund are of two kinds: the ordinary earnings supplement and the special earnings supplement.

Ordinary supplement. The ordinary supplement is available only

to manual workers. It allows them to draw up to 80 per cent
of basic earnings when they are temporarily laid off or when
they have worked fewer than their weekly contractual hours.
Normally this compensation is payable for a maximum of three
months, but in the public works building and building materials
sector the compensation period may be extended by periods of
three months up to a maximum not exceeding a quarter of the
time taken to complete the project on which they are working.
Approval must be sought from the Ministry of Labour.

New rules applying to the special supplement. Unlike the ordinary
supplement, the special supplement (also 80 per cent of basic
earnings) is payable to both blue- and white-collar workers, when
longer-term lay-offs or company restructuring take place. A law
passed in July 1991 revised the rules for its application. It is
the use of this fund which in the past often spiralled out of
control, with governments repeatedly allowing payments to be
extended well beyond the theoretical maximum period. The
most celebrated example was Fiat, where some 7,000 workers
were laid off for periods sometimes in excess of five years
while the company carried out extensive restructuring. Recourse
to the CIG allowed Fiat to modernize its plant, management
and industrial relations procedures without making the workers
redundant. They were either reabsorbed into their old jobs,
redeployed or, in some cases, retired. This machinery has been
extremely useful in enabling restructuring to be carried out in
industry without recourse to the large-scale redundancies which
would inevitably have ensued elsewhere, especially in view of the
virtual non-existence of unemployment benefit in Italy.

The new rules, however, aim to place limitations on the use
of the special supplement. First, it will apply only to firms with
more than fifteen employees. Second, restructuring exercises may
only last for a maximum of two years (with a maximum of two
extensions, lasting one year each) and firms in financial crisis will
only be entitled to *cassa* payments for a maximum of one year. In
both cases, each production unit will only be entitled to draw *cassa*
payments for up to thirty-six months in a five-year period. Lastly,
firms must use the principle of 'rotation', with penalties imposed
on those who do not. Rotation means that work must be delivered
by workers on a rota basis, i.e. the same group of workers must not

be laid off for continuous periods: instead, groups of workers must alternate.

Permission to use the special supplement fund must be sought from the regional labour inspectorate, and will be granted by the Ministry of Labour.

Transfer of undertakings

Italy has only recently implemented directive 771/187 on the transfer of undertakings, profoundly altering the previous legislation, article 2112 of the Civil Code. The new legislation, which came into force on 29 December 1990, states:

- Where a transfer of undertakings occurs, employment contracts shall continue uninterrupted and employees shall retain all their acquired rights.
- The new owner is also obliged to assume responsibility for all contractual entitlements at the time the take-over occurs.

The new owners are bound by the two obligations above unless able to release themselves according to sections 410 and 411 of the Code of Civil Procedure.

- The new owner is obliged to apply all collective agreements in force at the time of the take-over until such time as they expire unless they are replaced by other collective agreements applying to the new company.

In addition, the new law also requires the transferor and transferee of the company (with more than fifteen employees) to inform the relevant workers' representatives, as well as their trade unions, of the transfer at least twenty-five days in advance. The communication must state the reason for the transfer, its legal, economic and social consequences, and any possible measures which may affect employees.

The workers' representatives or their trade unions can request a joint examination of the transfer, provided they apply in writing within seven days of receiving the initial communication. The transferor and transferree are obliged to set the examination in motion within a further seven days. Regardless of the outcome, the consultation is deemed to be at an end after ten days.

Exceptions under the new law include firms which have been certified as being in a state of crisis by the CIPI (*Comitato Interministeriale per la Politica Industriale*) and those which have been officially declared bankrupt. In these circumstances the transferee is not obliged to take on the employment contracts of all employees. Excess employees will technically remain employed by the transferor, with the right to priority recruitment for one year, should the transferee need additional labour. However, the re-recruitment of former employees in the new company need not be according to the terms and conditions of their previous contracts.

Appendix

Ministry of Labour and Social
Security (Ministerio del Lavoro e
della Previdenza Sociale):
Via Flavia 6
00187 Roma
tel. + 39 6 4683

Employment Directorate
(Direzione Generale dei Rapporti
di Lavoro):
as for Ministry of Labour

AIDP (Italian personnel
managers' association):
Via Cornalia 19
20124 Milano
tel. + 39 2 67 09 558

Confindustria (central employers'
organization):
Viale dell'Astronomia 30
0100 Roma
tel. + 39 6 59031

Confederazione Generale Italiana
del Lavoro (CGIL)
Corso d'Italia, 25
00198 Roma
tel. + 39 6 84761

Confederazione Italiana Sindacati
Lavoratori (CISL)
Via Po, 21
00198 Roma
tel. + 39 6 84 73 1

Unione Italiana del Lavoro (UIL)
Via Lucullo, 6
00187 Roma
tel. + 39 6 49731

Federazione Nazionale Dirigenti
Aziende Industriali (FNDAI)
Via Palermo, 12
00184 Roma
tel. + 39 6 47 40 35 1/2/3/4

Federazione Nazionale Dirigenti
di Aziende Commerciali
Via Nazionale, 163
00184 Roma
tel. + 39 6 67 81 49 8

8

Netherlands

Dutch industrial relations are characterized by a high degree of consultation and consensus, resting on statutory powers of employee representation at establishment level. National tripartite and bipartite forums also act as an important means of generating consensus, although their influence on pay bargaining was much reduced during the 1980s. There is little detailed regulation on the status of trade unions and industrial action. The Netherlands has a less turbulent history of industrial relations in general than most other European countries, and the emphasis continues to be on not disrupting the relationship between the social partners.

National consultative machinery

The Economic and Social Council (*Sociaal-Economisch Raad*, SER) was set up in 1950 as a discussion forum and advisory body. The government is under a statutory obligation to seek the SER's advice on all proposals for major social and economic legislation. The SER is not obliged to adopt a unanimous position and its role is purely advisory. In addition to giving an opinion on legislative proposals, the SER is also charged with 'stimulating new developments in industry', monitoring occupational public law bodies, and directly participating in the implementation of some legislation. The SER has also served as a consensus-shaping forum on industrial relations and economic issues, such as youth training, but rarely on pay questions. It has a maximum of forty-five members, with equal numbers of employer representatives, employee representatives and independent experts appointed by the Crown, one of which chairs its monthly meetings. The president of the Nederlandsche Bank and the director of the Central Planning Bureau are *ex officio* members. Voting on issues tends to be *en bloc*, with Crown members often casting what is effectively the deciding vote.

The Labour Foundation (*Stichting van de Arbeid*, SA) was set up
in 1945 as a central bipartite forum for consultation and negotiation
between employers and trade unions. Its initial role was tailored to
the Netherlands' highly centralized wage-setting machinery in the
1950s, where it effectively jointly prepared a pay recommendation
subsequently adopted and implemented by government. Its current
role is concerned with reaching common positions on other aspects
of industrial relations, which may be expressed in non-binding
accords. The last accord in which pay played an important part was
the November 1982 framework accord on pay indexation and cuts in
working hours, agreed in the face of a possible statutory pay freeze.
Nevertheless, the government still looks to the foundation to come
up with a consensus position on pay in its autumn consultation. (The
foundation, which meets several times a year, also produces a spring
consultation document.)

In 1982 the foundation issued a set of recommendations on
recruitment and selection, again taking the place of statutory
intervention in this area. These so-called STAR recommendations
are dealt with in the first volume in the IDS/IPM European
Management Guides series, on recruitment. More recently the
foundation has come to agreements on the need to tackle
entitlement to disability benefit and absenteeism – though not
on the final action proposed by the government in the field of
disability benefit – and on unemployment among ethnic minorities.

Employee representation

Although Dutch trade unions have been seeking to establish trade
union delegations at the workplace, and obtain rights for workplace
union representatives (see below), the dominant form of employee
representation is through the statutory system of works councils. A
recent recommendation by the Economic and Social Council argued
for more precise definition and regulation of the rights of workplace
trade union delegations. There are also provisions for workers to
obtain places on the supervisory boards of companies.

Works councils

The statutory system of works councils (*ondernemingsraad*) has been developed through a number of legislative steps, beginning in 1950. Under the 1979 legislation (*Wet op de Ondernemingsraden*), most recently amended in 1990, works councils are employee-only bodies which must be established by the employer at enterprise level where certain size criteria are met (see below). The 1990 amendments were in part a response to a recommendation from the Economic and Social Council for a clarification of the differences between trade union and works council tasks.

Employers in any enterprise (*onderneming*) employing:

- At least 100 employees or
- At least thirty-five employees working more than one-third of normal full-time hours

are obliged to establish a works council. Employers who have two or more enterprises which meet these criteria may establish a joint works council where this is deemed appropriate to facilitate the application of the law. Conversely, the employer may also establish individual works councils for parts of an enterprise employing 100 or more employees. 'Enterprise' is defined as any 'organization operating . . . as an independent unit', and could therefore be taken to mean an individual workplace, office, shop or institution providing a service. The employer and the works council must meet at least six times a year, and discuss the operation of the enterprise in at least two of these meetings.

Special regulations apply to enterprises with fewer than 100 employees in the area of employees' eligibility for election, right to information and consultation, and the need for prior agreement (see below).

The costs of operating the works council are borne wholly by the employer. These expenses may include, if the works council wishes and provided the employer is notified in advance, the cost of obtaining expert advice and any costs incurred in legal proceedings taken by the works council.

Composition and election. Works councils consist solely of employees from the enterprise to which they relate, and are directly elected by all employees with at least six months' service (one year's where fewer than 100 employees are employed). Any employee with at least one year's service is eligible to stand for office. The size of council varies according to enterprise size, with three members where there are fewer than fifty employees, five members for 50–100 employees, seven members for 100–200 employees, up to thirteen members for enterprises with between 600 and 1,000 employees. An additional two members may be elected for each additional 1,000 employees, up to a maximum works council size of twenty-five.

Elections are held every three years on the basis of lists of candidates, although the works council itself may pass regulations varying the period of election to between two and four years or allowing half the council to step down every two years. Lists of candidates may be submitted by trade unions represented in the enterprise, or by non-unionized employees provided they account for a third of the work force and that a minimum quorum of thirty signatures is obtained. In practice, on average some 70 per cent of works council members are union-nominated. Provision may be made for separate lists for different groups within the work force, to ensure that the works council reflects different occupational groups, or other subdivisions of the work force deemed to be relevant.

Status and rights of works council members. Works council members may not be disadvantaged through their candidacy for or membership of a works council. Special dismissal protection also applies. Works council members' employment cannot be terminated except by mutual written consent or for an urgent reason which must be notified to the employee without delay, where the enterprise or department in which the employee works ceases operations, or for an 'important reason', provided it is submitted to a cantonal court. There is also protection for candidates and works council members for two years after their candidacy or membership: any termination of employment requires the permission of the cantonal court, which may consent only if it considers that the dismissal is unrelated to the employee's candidacy: the same provisos, including the possibility of termination of employment for 'an important reason', apply as in the case of current works council members.

Works councils meet during normal working hours, and works council members are entitled to paid time off to attend the meetings. Time off is also granted to allow participation in any other discussions required for the council to perform its duties or obtain information about employment conditions in the enterprise. The employer must also provide paid time off for works council members to attend training courses, with the precise amount of time off to be settled jointly between the works council and the employer. Time off for consultation may not be less than sixty hours a year, with at least five days annually for training.

Works council members, and any experts consulted by them, are bound by a requirement of confidentiality on business and industrial secrets as well as any issue which the employer or works council deems to be confidential: in general, an issue must be identified as confidential before being submitted for discussion, and where possible the precise scope of secrecy and the duration of confidentiality should be stated. Works council members continue to be bound when their period of office has expired.

Information rights. The employer is obliged to provide the works council with all information which can be reasonably required for it to carry out its tasks, in writing if requested. Specifically, this includes:

- The legal form of the employing organization, its articles of association, board members and parent company – together with details of its ownership and control, should the enterprise be a subsidiary or part of a group.
- Twice annually a report on the general conduct of the business, and specifically those matters on which the works council has a right of consultation or where its prior agreement is required (see below). This includes the employer's expectations for the future, and investments undertaken, both domestically and abroad.
- Annual accounts, backed up where appropriate by financial information on the individual enterprise if it is not readily identifiable from the published accounts.
- At least once annually, a report on employment trends in the enterprise and social policy in the preceding year, together with the employer's expectations for the coming year.

Consultation with the works council. Any consultation between the employer and the works council must take place at a time which allows the works council's opinion to have a 'significant impact' on any decision. Employers must provide information backed up by reasoned argument, and with an assessment of the implications of any decision for the work force. The main issues on which the employer is required to consult the works council are:

- Transfer of control of the enterprise or any part of it.
- Acquisitions, joint ventures, divestments.
- Closures or relocation.
- Significant reductions, expansion or other changes in the enterprise's activities, including major investments and loans.
- Recruitment of employees or the hiring of temporary staff.
- Commissioning of external expert advice by the employer, and the terms of reference of any consultancy hired.

If the advice of the works council is taken, the implementation of decisions generally runs very smoothly. Should the employer decide to reject the works council's position, the employer must set out the reasons in writing and may not proceed with the proposed action until after a delay of one month, unless otherwise agreed by the works council.

In cases of disagreement the works council has the right to lodge an appeal with the Companies Chamber of the Court of Appeal in Amsterdam, which can examine the issue and, if it deems the employer to have behaved unreasonably, enforce a rescission of the decision and prohibit the employer from proceeding further. Delays in the legal process are also substantial and the costs of the case have to be borne by the employer, including the cost of the works council's legal representation. In practice, this latent power creates the basis of negotiation between works council and employer, although in law works councils have no formal right to negotiate as such.

Works council prior agreement. The agreement (*instemming*) of the works council is required in the event of any employer decision to lay down, amend or withdraw provisions in the following areas, provided they are not already regulated by a collective agreement (see also below):

- Works regulations.

- Any arrangement on hours or holidays.
- A pay or job evaluation system.
- A pension, profit-sharing or savings scheme.
- Regulations on health and safety.
- Regulations on recruitment, dismissal, promotion, training and employee appraisal.
- Grievance procedures.
- Policy towards young employees.

The employer must submit the proposed decision in writing, together with the reasons, and any implications for the work force. The employer may appeal to a cantonal court if the works council withholds approval: the court will override the works council's refusal only if the refusal is unreasonable or if the employer can adduce 'important reasons'. Any decision taken without works council approval is null and void, provided the works council appeals within one month.

Works councils and collective agreements. No works council decision may contravene the provisions of a collective agreement, and works council approval is not required in areas already regulated by collective agreement. Some firms, such as Philips, which is covered by a company collective agreement, prefer to detail as much as possible in their collective agreement, although others, of which Royal Dutch Shell is one example, opt for a less specific collective agreement and more consultation with the works council at establishment level. Moreover, additional powers may be granted to a works council under the terms of a collective agreement, although not in regard to terms and conditions set out in that agreement.

Works councils cannot, by law, negotiate collective agreements, a prerogative reserved exclusively for trade unions.

Rights in smaller enterprises. Different provisions apply where the enterprise employs between thirty-five and 100 employees. A works council may be set up on a voluntary basis in enterprises employing between ten and thirty-five employees. However, if no works council is established, the employer must allow the work force the opportunity to meet at least twice a year, and report annually on the business. The main differences as regards works councils' powers in enterprises with thirty-five to 100 employees are:

- No right to commission expert advice without prior permission, unless the cost is met by the works council from its regular budget.
- No specified minimum time-off requirements.
- Consultation has to take place only if the proposed change might lead to job losses or a major change in conditions of employment affecting at least a quarter of the work force. The obligation to defer implementation of a decision is restricted to closures, significant reduction or expansion of activities, or relocation.
- Information may be presented orally.

Employee representation at board level

Since 1971 all public limited liability companies employing at least 100 workers and with a balance sheet total of Fl 22·5 million must establish a supervisory board (*raad van commissarissen*). In the event of a vacancy the supervisory board may co-opt a person proposed by the works council in the enterprise, though not an employee of the enterprise. Works councils also have a right to object to any appointment to the supervisory board, with disputes resolvable through the courts if necessary.

Trade unions

There are three recognized trade union centres:

- FNV (*Federatie Nederlandse Vakbeweging*) is the largest, with a total of approximately 1 million members, some 80 per cent of all Dutch trade unionists. The FNV was created through a merger of the Socialist Confederation (NVV) and the Catholic Confederation (NKV) which began in 1976 and was completed in 1982. The FNV consists of nineteen sectoral and occupational affiliate unions, the largest of which are: the public sector union AbvaKabo (281,000 members); the industrial union Industriebond FNV (217,000 members) and the construction workers' union Bouw- en Houtbond FNV (160,000 members).

- CNV (*Christelijk Nationaal Vakverbond*), the Protestant trade union centre, which had some 310,000 members in 1991. Like the FNV, it consists of sectoral and occupational affiliates.
- MHP (*Vakcentrale voor Middelbaar en Hoger Personeel*) represents white-collar and managerial employees and has 133,000 members in three functional affiliates.

A fourth centre, the AVC, which consists principally of civil servants, was established in 1990 but is not allowed to participate in organizations such as the SER or Labour Foundation until it has existed for two years and established itself as a representative organization.

Dutch unions are, therefore, not organized along political lines, have no political factions, and do not make electoral recommendations. However, there is correspondence between the stated aims of the FNV and those of the Labour Party (PvdA).

Trade union density is estimated at some 30 per cent of the labour force, compared with 40 per cent in 1975. Unionization levels were at a low point in the mid-1980s but have gradually picked up since then, with recruitment in sectors which have not traditionally been highly unionized such as financial services. There is no closed shop, though, for historical reasons, printing has 100 per cent membership.

There is little general statutory regulation of trade unions as such, and trade unions may be established by employees under the general principles of freedom of association. However, in order to sign collective agreements unions must have a legal personality, as well as specifying in their own rule books that they may bargain collectively. Only a trade union, as opposed to a works council, can negotiate a collective agreement. Unions enjoy some positive statutory rights in the area of collective dismissals.

A number of union rights and concessions are also regulated by collective agreement, such as workplace facilities, notice boards, time for members' meetings, etc. For example, the framework agreement in the insurance industry provides for the availability of rooms for meetings, notice boards, internal mail facilities, room on the employer's premises outside office hours for members' meetings, and a guarantee that no employee will be disadvantaged through exercising the duties of a trade union representative.

Trade unions draw up their own rules and regulations for

elections and voting procedures on strikes (see below), a freedom from statutory intervention which continues to be fiercely defended.

In contrast to members of works councils, official trade union representatives, registered as such with managements, are not specifically legally protected, although there may be provisions in collective agreements on their rights and status. Unions have been pressing for legislation and have been engaged in discussions with the government on the possibility of introducing statutory dismissal protection along the lines of the clauses for works council members.

Trade union representatives at company level may be called into collective bargaining at company or sectoral level, but their prime responsibility is to attend to the needs of individual members and act as a workplace base for the union. In practice, as noted above, about 70 per cent of all works council places are occupied by trade union candidates.

A recent Economic and Social Council recommendation called for more specific arrangements to be made regulating facilities for union representatives in the workplace.

Employers' organizations

As with Dutch trade unions, Dutch employers' organizations consist of a central confederation – though not a single one – with sectoral affiliates. The main organizations are the Confederation of Dutch Enterprises (*Verbond van Nederlandse Ondernemingen*, VNO); the Christian Employers' Confederation (*Nederlands Christelijk Werkgeversverbond*, NCW) and two organizations representing small and medium-size employers, KNOV and NCOV. The two most important are the VNO and the NCW, which in some cases have overlapping membership.

The VNO is the largest employer organization, with approximately 10,000 companies employing ten or more employees, most of which are affiliated through member federations. The two most significant are the FME, which represents employers in the metalworking and electrical engineering industries and includes the large concerns of Hoogovens and Philips, and the AWV, a general organization of some 350 firms, including Shell and Unilever.

All the employers' organizations share an umbrella organization, the RCO, which is located in the VNO's administrative head-quarters.

Collective bargaining

Over the last twenty years the Netherlands has moved from a highly centralized pay-setting and bargaining environment to a model built around sectoral and company bargaining. Coverage of the work force by collective agreement remains high, however, and some 75 per cent of private-sector employees fall under the scope of collective agreements.

Industry-level bargaining predominates, with agreements concluded between the appropriate affiliates of the union and employer centres. (Agreements will typically be signed by both FNV and CNV affiliates.) Collective agreements are frequently fleshed out at company level with the co-operation of works councils, which are, therefore, becoming increasingly if indirectly involved in discussions on the determination of agreed terms and conditions.

Company bargaining has developed in importance in recent years, and there are now some 650 company agreements covering 545,000 employees. Many of these are concentrated in the chemical industry, where there are no industry-level agreements, and companies such as Akzo, Shell, DSM and ICI all have house agreements. Large conglomerates, such as Hoogovens and Philips, also negotiate their own collective agreements.

Collective agreements

Two main laws regulate collective bargaining: the 1927 law on collective agreements (*Wet op de Collectieve Arbeidsovereenkomst*) and the 1937 law on the extension of collective agreements (*Wet op het Algemeen Verbindend en het Onverbindendverklaren van Bepalingen van Collectieve Arbeidsovereenkomsten*).

A collective agreement is defined as 'an agreement, entered into by one or more employers or one or more organizations with full legal rights of employers, and one or more organizations with full legal rights of employees, in which principally or exclusively terms and conditions of employment are regulated, which must be taken into account in employment contracts'. Collective agreements may also cover contracts for groups such as freelance or temporary and agency employees and can exclude certain employee categories, such as senior managers.

Organizations can be party to a collective agreement only if the statutes of the organization expressly provide for it. The law on collective agreements does not regulate how an organization may acquire the capacity to bargain collectively or what internal regulations it must have, for example on balloting to accept a settlement.

Collective agreements are legally binding where the employer is a member of a signatory organization or negotiates a company agreement (see also below). Breaches of the agreement may be punishable by fines. Agreements must be centrally registered, and do not come into force until they are.

'Minimum conditions' laid down in the collective agreements can be improved on but may not be worsened in individual contracts of employment. These typically refer to pay levels, annual holidays, etc. 'Standard conditions' may not be altered at all in individual contracts and would include elements such as the 'peace clause' prohibiting industrial action during the lifetime of an agreement.

Extension of agreements

The Minister of Social Affairs can declare certain clauses of a collective agreement binding on all employers and employees in a given branch even if they are not members of a signatory organization. Extension may follow at the request of one or more parties to a collective agreement and must concern terms in a collective agreement which the Minister holds to be of importance for the 'majority of employees in a given industry'.

Only the so-called normative clauses of a collective agreement, that is, those sections regulating pay, hours and other terms, can be made generally binding. Procedural aspects or other obligations, such as a requirement that the parties refrain from industrial action, cannot be extended. The Minister must seek the opinion of the Labour Foundation before extending an agreement.

Industrial action

The Netherlands is notable for its industrial harmony – vying with Germany for the lowest incidence of industrial action in the European Community. In 1987 thirteen days were lost per thousand employees, compared with 163 in the UK, 278 in Italy and, in that year, two in Germany. There is no legislation governing industrial action. The rights of association and assembly are laid down in articles 8 and 9 of the constitution, and the right to strike is based on article 5 of the European Social Charter, which was ratified by the Dutch government in 1980, and on the courts applying and developing general legal principles.

Strikes

As collective agreements are binding, strike action directed at the terms of an existing agreement is unlawful.

There is no statutory requirement to give notice of strike action and no definition of any period of notice. However, in practice, failure to give 'adequate notice' can result in the loss of support and sympathy from employees and the general public. More important, it could also result in the courts ruling the strike illegal on the grounds that it is 'premature' (*voorbarigheid*) or 'unconsidered' (*onzorgvuldigheid*). There is a presumption that strikes should constitute a last resort in the event of a collective dispute, and action must also be 'proportionate' to the objectives pursued. (This argument has been used to challenge the legality of go-slows, on the grounds that employees can continue to draw pay whilst inflicting economic damage on the employer.)

Ballots are governed by the trade unions' internal regulations. Generally, rejection of a settlement requires a two-thirds majority and a vote for strike action a three-quarters majority.

There are no specific statutory definitions of permitted or prohibited forms of industrial action. 'Purely' political strikes are not protected under the charter and are hence illegal. Actions such as blockades or occupations run the risk of being ruled illegal by the courts as 'actions contrary to the rights and freedoms of others'. Sympathy action may also founder on the grounds that the rights of a third party, the employer indirectly affected, are harmed. However, sympathy strikes may be allowed in so far as terms and conditions of employment in one sector could affect those in another. Port blockades may be ruled illegal also, on the grounds of national interest.

Unofficial action may be ruled unlawful by the courts and wildcat strikes are frequently taken over by the unions to protect their members. This is particularly true in the ports and in the construction industry. Trade unions can be held liable for damages resulting from any industrial action found illegal.

An employer has the right to seek a court injunction to prevent a strike, but as long as the strike falls within the charter's guidelines, or Dutch law in general, it is unlikely to be granted. There are often clauses in a collective agreement prohibiting certain actions, and trade unions are obliged to ensure that their members abide by the terms and conditions of a collective agreement.

Participation in a strike suspends the contract of employment but does not constitute grounds for termination. Disciplinary action against striking employees is deemed illegal if the strike action was not ruled illegal in a court of law. In cases of unlawful action, a trade union can be held liable for damages if a strike is ruled to be illegal and the union nevertheless proceeds with the action, although it is not clear from case law whether this would apply in retrospect to an action already begun but then ruled as unlawful.

Lock-outs

Lock-outs are an extreme rarity, and under the Civil Code an employer would have to continue paying employees if work was not possible owing to action on the part of the employer.

Conciliation and arbitration

There is no public conciliation or arbitration service for the private sector, although in 1986 a number of independent experts were nominated by the Labour Foundation to whom disputes may be referred on a voluntary basis. Collective agreements may stipulate an arbitration mechanism, including an agreed list of arbitrators, and detail procedures to be followed. These cover primarily issues arising out of the interpretation of agreements rather than disputes arising during the renegotiation of terms.

Collective dismissal

Collective dismissals are governed principally by the 1976 law on the registration of collective dismissals (*Wet Melding Collectieve Ontslag*), and by relevant references in the Civil Code. A collective dismissal is defined as the dismissal of at least twenty employees over a period of three months within the catchment area of a single regional labour exchange (*gewestelijke arbeidsbureau*, GAB). Collective dismissals can also be covered by collective agreements, where a narrower definition may be adopted. For example, in the 1990 collective agreement in the textile industry collective dismissal is defined as the dismissal of at least 10 per cent of the work force (with a minimum of ten employees) or the dismissal of twenty-five employees regardless of the size of the work force.

Under the 1976 law, prior notification of a collective dismissal must be handed in writing both to a trade union with members among the work force and to the regional labour exchange (GAB). Although no specific period of notice is detailed in the law (this may be detailed under a collective agreement), the law does say that notice must be given as early as possible once a decision has been made regarding which individual employees are affected. In companies where a works council is in existence, the council has to be notified of any imminent collective dismissal and allowed to present its advice prior to a final decision or the implementation of the collective dismissal. (Works councils must also be consulted prior to any mergers, and must be kept up to date on the economic development of the company.)

There is a standard one-month delay between the notification of a collective dismissal to the GAB and the GAB's initiation of the legally required dismissal authorization, except in the event of bankruptcy. The GAB has to investigate ways of preventing the collective dismissal and mitigating its effect on the work force. The GAB is entitled to access to the advice given by the works council, although there is no legal requirement stipulating the precise contents of the consultation process for collective dismissals with the works council. The GAB can (and often does) delay the dismissal authorization if it judges that insufficient consultation with the works council has taken place.

Although there is no statutory provision for redundancy payments (see 'individual termination' in the second volume of the
European Management Guides, series, *Terms and Conditions of
Employment*), a number of collective agreements incorporate
clauses covering extra redundancy payments in the case of collective
dismissal. The textile agreement provides for a guaranteed minimum
one-off payment for employees aged between 40 and 65 years,
ranging from one week's salary for 40–44-year-olds with between one
and nine years' service to thirteen weeks' salary for employees aged
60–64 with more than thirty years' service. At Unilever any redundancies experienced by employees under 58 years old and caused by
'restructuring' will entitle those affected to an extra payment of
between 2 per cent and 10 per cent of annual salary, depending on
length of service. Payments may be settled during negotiations with
works councils over the implementation of collective dismissals.
They may take the form of additions to unemployment benefit.

A government survey carried out in 1989 on redundancy
payments in cases of collective dismissal showed that most
payments were dependent on the age of the employee and length
of service, and that the majority of collectively agreed payments
took the form of a percentage of final salary in a one-off payment.

Transfer of undertakings

Transfer of undertakings is covered by the law on transfer
of undertakings (*Wet Overgang van Ondernemingen*), which
implements the EC directive. Under the law the new employer
is bound to the terms and conditions of any existing collective
agreement. Change of ownership is not grounds for termination
of contract. Under the terms of the works council law, works
councils must be informed of proposed transfers of ownership
in sufficient time to allow the works council's opinion to have a
'significant impact' on the final decision. The Economic and Social
Council has also agreed a code of practice dealing with mergers
of companies employing more than 100 staff. However, this is not
legally binding unless incorporated in a collective agreement. The
provisions require all mergers to be registered with any relevant
trade unions, which have a right to reply to merger proposals and to
negotiate on behalf of employees. Failure to consult could lead the

Economic and Social Council to issue a so-called public declaration of reprimand which could prejudice the completion of the merger.

Appendix

The Ministry of Social Affairs
and Employment (Ministerie
van Sociale Zaken en
Werkgelegenheid):
Postbus 20801
2600 EV Den Haag
tel. +31 70 371 5911
fax +31 70 371 4555

Dutch Association of Personnel
Managers, Nederlandse
Vereniging van
Personeelsbeleid, NVP):
Catharijnensingel 53
Postbus 19124
3501 DC Utrecht
tel. +31 30 367101 (membership
enquiries), 367155 (training),
367137 (administration)

VNO
Postbus 93093
2509 AB Den Haag
tel. + 31 70 3497373

FNV
Postbus 8456
1005 AL Amsterdam
tel. + 31 20 581 6300
fax + 31 20 684 4541

Social and Economic Council
(Commissie Ontwikkeling
Bedrijven van de
Sociaal-Economische Raad,
COB/SER):
Postbus 90405
2509 LK Den Haag
tel. +31 70 3499 499

Stichting van de Arbeid
(Labour Foundation):
Postbus 90405
2509 LK Den Haag
tel. +31 70 349 9648

Netherlands–British Chamber of
Commerce:
Holland Trade House
Bezuidenhoutseweg 181
2594 AH Den Haag
tel. +31 70 478881
fax +31 70 477975

9

Portugal

An understanding of Portuguese industrial relations demands a general appreciation of the developments over the last twenty years which have fundamentally shaped the system and its actors. Under the Salazar dictatorship (1932–68) there was no right of association or freedom to bargain. Corporate trade unions were the only organizations purporting to represent employees; their leaders had to be officially approved and their finances were controlled by the state. The situation eased slightly during the Caetano administration from 1968 to 1974, when limited collective bargaining was introduced, providing a fillip to trade union organization and giving rise to the unofficial formation of the Intersindical trade union co-ordinating structure, a grouping of some thirty trade unions encompassing various political persuasions. The 1974 revolution, spearheaded by the Armed Forces Movement, saw factory occupations and the ousting of some senior personnel, including trade union officials, associated with the former regime – events in which the Communist Party, emerging into the open, took an active role. A wholesale nationalization programme, embracing key sectors such as banking and insurance, road haulage and shipping, was launched by a government of the Armed Forces Movement, headed by General Vasco Gonçalves. A Socialist government was subsequently elected in the first general election.

A new constitution conferred many basic guarantees upon workers and trade unions – notably the rights to work, to organize collectively, to be represented at the workplace and to strike. Workers were also given the right to be consulted over employment legislation. The body of legislation promulgated between 1975 and 1979 fleshed out these basic rights. In addition to approving laws which were favourable to employees, the government also shared and promoted trade union interests in other spheres. During this period an atmosphere of mutual antagonism built up between unions and employers.

On accession to the European Community in 1986 there was broad recognition of the imperative to modernize an economy weakened by fifty years of fascism and the impact of recent colonial wars. This went hand in hand with a realization of the need to foster more constructive dialogue between the social partners and propel the labour relations environment closer to what was seen in Portugal as the EC 'norm'. In 1989 the constitution was amended by the newly elected Social Democrats which paved the way for a privatization programme and other liberalization measures necessitated by the approaching single European market.

Of Portugal's 10 million population, around 4·8 million are economically active, 2·8 million as wage and salary earners. The official national-unemployment rate stands at around 5 per cent, with approximately a further 18 per cent of workers in some form of precarious (temporary) employment. At least 80 per cent of the working population are employed in firms with fewer than ten staff and only 4 per cent in 'large' companies with more than 200 employees. Thus industrial relations has been characterized, on the one hand, by large, often publicly owned, companies with strong employee representation and managements which frequently include political appointees. On the other hand are numerous small private firms, frequently family-run, where worker representation is weak. Union density is variously put at 40–50 per cent of the work force.

National-level consultation

There is no tradition of regular independent contact between employers and trade unions, and certainly no bipartite nationwide bargaining. In any event, union confederations have no power to conclude legally binding collective agreements. According to one senior personnel manager, 'Portugal has the most complete set of labour laws in Europe – which are often not observed.' Certainly, the extent of labour legislation has served to inhibit the development of collective bargaining, which is still a highly political process. As a consequence, many collective agreements contain little more than the statutory provisions. The paucity of content is recognized by the latest Economic and Social Agreement (see below), which supports the extension of bargaining in both quantitative and qualitative terms. Some commentators would like to see framework laws supplemented by collective agreements but this would require a greater commitment to the bargaining process than has developed to date.

Permanent Council of Social Consultation

The tripartite Permanent Council for Social Consultation (*Conselho Permanente de Concertação Social*) was established by statute in 1984 to promote dialogue between the social partners at national level on all social and economic matters. It holds regular meetings either in full session or in working groups. Currently there are separate divisions dealing with economic and employment matters, though its consultation base may shortly be extended to include representation of family and consumer interests. The council comprises six government ministers, including the Prime Minister, three representatives of each of the two trade union confederations, the CGTP and UGT, and two members each from the three national employers' organizations.

Economic and Social Pact

A change in the industrial relations climate is evidenced by the more active role now being played by the council, which produced an Economic and Social Pact (*Acordo Económico e Social*, AES) for 1991, outlining a commitment as well as concrete measures to transform the economy, protect the competitiveness of industry and improve citizens' living standards. The agreement also contains proposals for a limited programme of new legislation such as on vocational training, the modification of existing statutes (including plans to render the collective bargaining system more efficient and speed up the resolution of disputes) and the conclusion of agreements in the health and safety, social security and education and training areas. Enhancing the skills profile of the work force is seen as a key element in improving economic performance; around 20 per cent of the population are still estimated to be illiterate, and only 40 per cent of young people stay in education beyond 14 years of age.

Despite the conclusion of several past pacts, the latest agreement is seen as particularly important, even though the largest union confederation, the communist-oriented CGTP, and the agricultural employers declined to sign it. However, the two employers' confederations representing industry and commerce and the socialist-oriented UGT, the other union confederation, were signatories. Employers are hoping to secure greater work-force flexibility through a liberalization of employment legislation, particularly in areas such as the use of temporary contracts and grounds for dismissal. Trade unions, on the other hand, are seeking to defend rights acquired since the revolution as well as participating in the necessary process of change. One principal reason for the UGT's endorsement of the accord was to enhance its role as a social partner. Against this the CGTP's refusal turned on doubts as to whether its pay policy could guarantee the maintenance of living standards, against a background of high inflation and the lack of any mechanism for indexing pay. This difference between the two confederations goes to the very heart of Portugal's dilemma and serves to clarify some of the conflicts within the industrial relations system itself. The late 1980s boom has benefited some sections of the work force, but a substantial proportion remain on minimum wages supplemented by large amounts of overtime.

Other tripartite national bodies exist in the fields of vocational training, social security, health and safety and equal opportunities for women and men.

Participation in the formulation of labour legislation

Enterprise-based workers' committees and trade union organizations have a legal right to participate in the preparation of labour legislation, according to Article 56 of the Constitution. (Since Portugal has adopted ILO convention 113, the government also has an obligation to consult employers on these matters.) No proposal for legislation can be discussed or adopted by the government, national or regional assemblies unless employees' organizations have first had the chance to give their views. In the case of labour legislation, draft proposals are published as a supplement to the employment gazette *Boletim do Trabalho e Emprego*. Interested parties have thirty days to submit their responses. Trade union confederations tend to make extensive submissions, which are supported by individual affiliated unions. Early in 1991 the CGTP confederation alleged that legislation proposed under the 1991 Economic and Social Agreement was unconstitutional, as the consultation procedure had not been fully observed – a view shared by the Constitutional Court.

Enterprise-based employee consultation

Among the first actions taken by the Revolutionary Council was the publication in 1975 of three decree laws regulating trade union and industrial relations activity. The first of these recognized the CGTP–Intersindical as the national union confederation for employees, and was later rescinded when trade union plurality was recognized. The second concerned trade union organization generally and in particular the exercise of trade union rights within the enterprise. The third related to employers' rights to organize to defend their interests. Both these latter Acts remain in force (and are discussed below). Workers committees were recognized by the constitution. The law also recognizes the right of workers to elect a board member in publicly owned companies but it has rarely been exercised.

Demarcation between consultation and bargaining roles

Because grass-roots trade union organization really took off only towards the end of the decade, between 1975 and 1979 enterprise workers' committees often initially fulfilled both a consultative and a bargaining role – as some still do informally today. In 1979 a clear demarcation of functions was recognized in law, with trade unions being legally recognized as sole bargaining agents of employees at all levels, and workers committees, intended to promote democratic participation in the enterprise, granted extensive rights to information, consultation and supervision. In contrast to some other EC countries, there is little overlap in membership of enterprise workers' committees and trade union committees. This is partly due to the rather patchy coverage of both type of committee. However, where both types of committee exist there is often close liaison between them.

Workers' committees

Article 54 of the constitution establishes the right to set up workers' committees (*commissões de trabalhadores*) at enterprise level for the general purpose of defending workers' interests and promoting democratic participation in the enterprise. (It does not place an obligation on the employer to ensure that such a committee is established but once set up they must ensure it can function normally.) The legal framework on the constitution and functioning of the committees is provided by law 46/79 of 12 September 1979. Around 3,000 workers' committees are registered with the Ministry of Labour.

Composition. Legislation sets no lower limit on the size of enterprise in which a committee may be established. It does, however, set a maximum limit on the size of the committee, as follows:

- A three-member committee for undertakings with fewer than 201 employees.
- Between three and five for firms with 201 to 500 employees.
- Between five and seven for firms with 501 to 1,000 employees.
- Between seven and eleven for firms with 1,000 or more employees.

Where an undertaking has fewer than ten employees and annual sales do not exceed Esc 30 million (£116,000) the committee can comprise just two members.

There is a legal entitlement to set up establishment sub-committees of equivalent size with mandated powers in multi-establishment companies and, where appropriate, co-ordinating committees on which those elected from individual workers' committees sit.

Election. Trade unions hold no monopoly on presenting electoral lists and in fact may not draw up lists in their capacity as unions. However, they are often associated with specific lists. Candidacies must be endorsed by 10 per cent or 100 of the firm's permanent work force, every member of which has a right to stand for election. Only permanent staff are entitled to vote, the vote being conducted by direct secret ballot. Elected members enjoy the same right to protection against dismissal as trade union representatives (see below). The standing orders of the workers' committees which deal with such matters as the length of the terms of office and election arrangements must also be approved by employees, according to guidance laid down by the legislation.

Rights. Within the enterprise itself, a workers' committee has entitlements to be informed, to consultation and to supervise management. In practice this latter right does not, and under the law may not, impinge on the day-to-day management of the enterprise. The exercise of these rights also depends on the capacity of the committee to carry them out. The law gives a workers' committee the right to:

- Receive all information necessary to carry out its functions.
- Oversee the management of the enterprise (*exercer o controlo de gestão nas respetivas empresas*).
- Participate in the reorganization of production activities.
- Manage the enterprise's social welfare funds.

Committee members are bound by secrecy on issues which management must not only state to be but also justify as confidential; they must also refrain from intervening in the day-to-day running of the enterprise. Each member has up to fifty hours' time off a month (if sitting on a co-ordinating committee) to fulfil their duties. Meetings with management must take place at least once a month, normally at the behest of the workers' committee itself.

Information. The kind of information which must be, and normally is, provided includes such items as operating plans and budgets, sales forecasts and volumes, the profit and loss account and balance sheet, internal works rules (including rules on working time arrangements often taken direct from sectoral agreements), the organization of production and the use of capital and labour, productivity and absenteeism levels and details of the total wage bill and its breakdown by grade. (By law firms have to publicize individual pay information, except for board members, on an annual basis.)

Consultation. The committee's views must be sought in writing when there are plans to close the company down or file for bankruptcy, relocate, reduce the size of the work force, worsen working conditions, change holiday schedules, change criteria regarding professional qualifications, job classification and promotions, or launch a financial recovery plan.

Supervision. In practice, powers giving committees the opportunity to supervise the management of a company are rarely exercised, except with regard to the enterprise's social welfare funds. However, committees often criticize management either directly or in circulars addressed to employees.

Bargaining. Although workers' committees are not legally recognized as bargaining agents, there are situations where they are engaged in informal negotiations in private companies such as to supplement terms, particularly pay, set in sectoral agreements. Some private employers in particular prefer to deal with workers' committees, which they see as a useful channel of communication where there is less scope for political conflict, compared with negotiating with trade unions. Sometimes this means the role of the committee is enhanced so as to marginalize the activity of on-site trade union committees.

There is no local tradition of quality circles or total quality management, and such bodies are mostly confined to foreign-owned companies.

Trade unions

Article 55 of the Constitution recognizes trade union freedom and gives workers the right to belong – or indeed not to belong – to trade unions of their choice. This contrasts with the pre-revolutionary situation in which trade union membership was compulsory (with dues deducted from pay at source) except in specific sectors where it was expressly forbidden. Unions are free to constitute themselves as they wish, make their own rules, exercise their rights within the enterprise and sign binding collective agreements, provided they are registered as unions with the Ministry of Labour and their rules comply with legal requirements. No representativity criteria exist. After registration they acquire a legal personality and could sue or be sued, although in practice this does not occur.

Two union confederations

There are two trade union confederations, organized according to political outlook, both of which stress independence from the state, employers and political parties – as well as a host of independent trade unions organized along either occupational or industry lines. According to a recent unpublished Ministry of Labour report, trade union density has dropped to around 42 per cent of the labour force, with 57 per cent of the union members in CGTP–Intersindical, 33 per cent in the UGT and 10 per cent in autonomous unions (see below). There are no official up-to-date figures on union membership but density is greatest among less skilled industrial employees, in large publicly owned enterprises and in the public services. Membership among white-collar, technical and managerial staff and among young people is low.

The Confederação Geral dos Trabalhadores Portugueses–Intersindical Nacional (CGTP–IN) was formed in 1970 during the Caetano period as the clandestine Intersindical, a loose umbrella grouping of thirty trade unions, influenced by various political currents, including that of the then banned Communist Party. After the revolution in 1975, the Intersindical was initially recognized as the sole national trade union confederation representing workers. Subsequently trade union pluralism was recognized by the constitution, and CGTP–Intersindical Nacional was established in 1977. It claims 1·1 million members. The dominant tendency within the CGTP is now communist – with an interchange of officials between the confederation and the party – but other political influences remain important.

Among the main planks of the CGTP–IN's philosophy are defence of collective rights, including the right to work, the improvement of living and working conditions, backed up where necessary by action, social solidarity, and emancipation of the working class. Its structure reflects both vertical and horizontal organization and encompasses federations representing industrial unions, district unions grouping together trade unions in the same geographical area, and occupational unions. The confederation co-ordinates and supports the activities of affiliated unions and provides legal services to assist in industrial disputes.

In 1978 the socialist-oriented União Geral de Trabalhadores (UGT) was formed and now claims 1 million workers. The principles espoused by the UGT emphasize the active participation of workers in union activity and the democratization of union structures as well as the right to work and to an equitable wage, equal opportunities, the social integration of workers, and action to eradicate regional disparities. The UGT has been the main proponent of a 'social contract for modernization' which ultimately led to the conclusion of the Economic and Social Agreement for 1991 (see above). Its structure is mainly vertical although some white-collar and technical occupational unions are affiliated. This means that in some enterprises there is sometimes more than one UGT union present.

Inter-confederal relations

The formation of the UGT broke CGTP–Intersindical's trade union monopoly and relationships since that time have been saddled by the consequent legacy of bitterness. Initially, at least, managements preferred to deal with unions not affiliated to a communist-dominated confederation and tended to concede more favourable agreements with UGT unions. It also suited government to deal with unions which were more prone to conclude agreements. However, there is now less rivalry between them and closer liaison both on tripartite bodies and on collective bargaining matters. Often joint talks take place before negotiations begin, both at sectoral and at company level. Many commentators believe that changes in the philosophy and tactics within the trade union confederations will prove pivotal to the future of Portuguese industrial relations.

Trade union committees

According to the law (decree 519 C1/79 on collective labour relations) only individual trade unions (as opposed to confederations) which are formally registered with the Ministry of Labour can negotiate and conclude collective agreements on behalf of employees, either at sectoral or at enterprise level.

Any such trade union has a right to organize within a firm as individual representatives, as a committee or as a joint committee (*delegados sindicais, comissões sindicais e comissões intersindicais*). There are no representativity criteria in terms of the right to be recognized nor any restriction on the size of committee, although there are limits in terms of the number of officials permitted paid time off for trade union duties – up to six in a firm with 499 staff (or more in larger concerns). Normally union members elect their workplace representatives according to internal union rules and inform management either directly or through full-time officials. Elected union representatives (and workers' committee members) enjoy enhanced protection against dismissal for their term of office and for the following five years. They also have up to five hours' time off (eight hours' for a member of a joint committee) per month to discharge their duties. A management is likely to conduct negotiations separately with two or more union committees, owing to the fact that employees may be members of different unions, which are affiliated to either of the major confederations or are independent. However, although union autonomy is jealously guarded, there are examples of joint union negotiating committees at both sectoral and company level. The law outlines the procedure for opening negotiations (see below), and although it obliges employers to engage in negotiations there is no obligation to reach agreement. The text of separately negotiated agreements (to be applied to employees affiliated to a particular union) may be identical or can contain different provisions.

Employers' associations

Again the law defines the rights of employers to organize in defence of and to promote the interests of their own enterprises. They may organize in a federal, union, confederal or category structure and are entitled to elaborate their own statutes and standing orders. They must register with the Ministry of Labour. The law invests both individual employers as well as employers' associations and confederations with the capacity to conclude binding collective agreements.

There are two main employers' confederations representing the interests of non-agricultural employers. The Confederação de Indústria Portuguesa (CIP) represents employers grouped into federations for the same industry or sector, as well as individually affiliated employers, together employing around 750,000 workers in the public sector and private companies, and comprising both large and small firms. The CIP's membership covers all main sectors of the economy, including industry, engineering, food, textiles, chemicals and transport. The Confederação do Comércio Português (CCP) represents both large and small firms in trade and commerce. The Confederação dos Agricultores de Portugal (CAP) represents employers in agriculture and exercises an influence on medium-sized and family-run enterprises. The confederations' main objectives are to represent employers as a whole in national-level discussions, on national tripartite bodies, with government and to provide legal assistance and support in collective negotiations.

Generally, many employers, particularly in the private sector, feel they have been operating in a difficult environment since the revolution. They claim that new labour legislation has given workers rights which are far better than the EC 'norm' but these provisions have proved inflexible in terms of creating the changes which are needed in the economy.

Bargaining

The bargaining system is highly fragmented, with no overriding pattern by level or subject matter. An individual contract of employment cannot contain provisions which are less favourable than those provided for by any collective contract or under statute, but can lay down more advantageous terms for the employee.

Agreements

Decree law 519 C1/79 governs collective bargaining at all levels in the private sector and in publicly owned enterprises. Agreements, which must be in writing and signed by the parties, are legally binding on their signatories and on organizations affiliated to them. In certain circumstances (see below) they may be extended to non-signatory parties. Agreements become valid once they have been registered with the Ministry of Labour and published in its official bulletin, the *Boletim do Trabalho e Emprego*. However, in publicly owned enterprises the approval of the minister covering the particular sector, as well as of those of the Ministries of Finance and Labour are needed, a bureaucratic procedure which is under review. Information on collective agreements and their coverage can be supplied by the Labour Ministry.

Apart from clauses on pay and other remuneration elements,

which may be reviewed annually, an agreement must last at least two years and remains in force until replaced by a new one. This must by law contain terms which are 'globally' more favourable than in the previous accord; while individual terms fixed in a collective agreement can be reduced, the new agreement must specify that overall terms are more favourable than in the agreement it replaces. Some employers feel this blocks more flexibility and innovation, though there are examples of agreements where acquired rights, such as seniority bonuses, are being bought out. Many agreements, particularly those at company level, cover blue and white-collar employees, sometimes up to quite senior levels.

Although government is still seen as a necessary catalyst to implement tripartite agreements by legislative rather than collectively agreed means, around 80 per cent of employees are covered by some form of collective agreement.

Levels of bargaining

The definition of a collective agreement according to type of accord is principally a technical matter depending on the identity of the bargaining parties and does not necessarily give a precise indication of its coverage.

Sectoral and company-level bargaining

Collective employment agreements (*contratos colectivos de trabalho*, CCT) are concluded between employers' associations and trade unions and cover most major sectors or industries with a national, or sometimes a regional, scope. The metalworking and chemicals agreements are national, whereas in textiles and banking and insurance there are separate regional agreements for the north and south of the country. There are normally separate agreements for the islands of Madeira and the Azores.

Collective employment accords (*acordos colectivos de trabalho*, ACT) are concluded between trade unions and employers for several companies either in the same geographical area or in the same sector. Enterprise agreements (*acordos de empresa*, AE) are concluded between unions and an employer for a single company, normally publicly owned, or large firms in the private sector. Both employers and trade unions may apply through an adherence agreement (*acordo de adesão*) to be covered by the terms of a published collective agreement. The pace of company bargaining may be expected to accelerate in future, owing to privatization and changes in the structure of the economy.

The existence of trade union plurality introduces a complicating factor into the bargaining arena. It means that more than one collective agreement may be concluded for the same area of activity or indeed within the same company – one signed by employers with the CGTP–IN-affiliated union, one with the UGT affiliate and perhaps others with non-affiliated unions. The texts of agreements may be identical or may contain differences. Although there is no tradition of joint union bargaining, it does occur, particularly in public companies. If agreements are overlapping, there is a convention that the accord favoured by the trade union representing the most members at the particular level will take precedence.

Extension of agreements

After consultations with the appropriate trade union and employers, the Ministry of Labour may decide to extend all or part of a collective agreement (either a CCT or an ACT) by means of an extension order (*portaria de extensão*, PE) to firms in the same sector not affiliated to signatory organizations. The ministry may also extend agreements to other sectors where conditions are similar if there are no parties capable of bargaining. If there is more than one agreement for the same sector of activity, the law gives no guidance on which should be extended. In the past, agreements covering particular occupations were extended. However, there is now a tendency to extend CCTs with a vertical coverage; the government believes a strong sectoral coverage of agreements is crucial where there are many small firms. The AES (see pages 172–3) contains proposals to speed up the extension procedure, although the government and trade unions would, if possible, prefer to see bargaining.

Regulation of employment conditions

The ministry also has the option of regulating labour conditions in unorganized sectors where it may be inappropriate to extend an existing agreement or in situations where there is a refusal to bargain or a delay in conducting negotiations. Such regulation is effected by a regulation of work order (*portaria de regulamentação de trabalho*, PRT). Initially, after the revolution, this procedure was often supported by the trade unions but is rarely used now and may be virtually phased out by legislation under discussion, except where there are genuinely no bargaining parties. Refusal to bargain would be dealt with by conciliation.

The bargaining procedure

The actual bargaining procedure is also laid down by the 1979 collective bargaining law. It must commence with a written proposal, usually initiated by a trade union and addressed to the other party, to conclude an agreement or review an existing accord. Details of clauses to be reviewed must be given. A reply in the form of a counter-proposal must be forthcoming within thirty days. Proposal and response must be submitted to the Ministry of Labour and supported by any appropriate data required by the bargaining parties. Talks must open within fifteen days of the receipt of the reply, except by mutual consent, otherwise the initiator may refer the matter to the ministry for conciliation. At the first meeting a written timetable for negotiations must be agreed and an exchange of powers of attorney between the parties must take place.

The law on industrial action

Strikes

The right to strike is guaranteed by Article 57 of the Constitution and applies to the private and public sectors. Lock-outs are expressly forbidden. Workers hold the sole right to define the scope of the interests to be defended by them. The lawfulness of strikes can only be evaluated by the labour courts, and there is a body of case law on the subject. Generally speaking, most disputes, including solidarity strikes, are lawful, so long as the decision is taken by properly constituted bodies, and the action is taken in pursuit of socio-economic goals, involving no attack on the organs of state or the constitution. Decree law 65/77 (26 August 1977) deals with industrial action. There are no reliable statistics but strikes were most frequent in the late 1970s and have reduced since the signing of the AES in October 1990. Public-sector disputes often take place before talks begin or to put pressure on negotiators, including government, during negotiations.

The decision to strike may be taken only by a trade union (in which case it would be bound by its own rules) or, if there is no union organization, by a meeting called by 20 per cent of the work force or 200 of the employees involved. In the latter circumstances a valid decision to strike would need to be taken at a meeting attended by a majority of workers, a simple majority of whom supported the strike vote by secret ballot. There are two conditions to be fulfilled once a strike has been declared.

- The employer and the Ministry of Labour must be given forty-eight hours' notice of the strike – five days in the case of essential services. This is normally observed, because days taken off work without justification can, once a certain limit has been reached, be used as grounds for individual dismissal. (In addition, the trade trade unions are aware that Portuguese strike law is among the most favourable in Europe towards workers, so they stick by the rules of the game.)
- Strikers must either be represented by a trade union or, if unorganized, must elect a strike committee from among their number.

Forms of action

Employees are free to determine their form of industrial action and, as noted above, have typically favoured tactics which minimize loss of earnings. A trade union or strikers' committee may organize pickets to persuade other workers to join the dispute provided it is done by peaceful means so as to preserve the constitutional right of other employees to work. Employers are not allowed to substitute other workers for employees on strike. However, it has been known in the public sector for management to use subcontracted services. Unions would not normally discipline their members for refusing to participate in a dispute, except possibly if the individual was an elected representative.

The individual contract of employment and the right to payment are suspended for employees directly involved in a dispute. On resumption of work there is deemed to be no break in continuity of service. Returning strikers may not be discriminated against. Since money is lost, and most unions have no strike fund, workers tend to engage in forms of action such as rolling strikes which cause the most disruption but involve the smallest loss of pay. Many employers pay their employees an attendance/assiduity bonus, often equivalent to around 10 per cent of normal pay, which is also lost in the event of a strike. Unions are also anxious not to jeopardize the position of temporary workers, who are particularly vulnerable in a dispute.

In the event of a dispute a minimum service – which is as yet undefined in law – must be guaranteed in certain specified industries, including posts and telecommunications, funeral services and water utilities. The government has special mobilization and requisition powers. Otherwise, there is a general obligation to assure the security of the workplace and maintenance of essential equipment during a dispute.

The law imposes fines ranging from Esc 50,000 to Esc 500,000 (£195–£1,950) for infringement of the strike law by both employers and strikers plus the possibility of a prison sentence should an employer impose a lock-out.

Dispute resolution

Conflicts of rights

A collective agreement must outline arrangements for monitoring compliance with its terms (questions of rights) and provide for the establishment of an 'interpretation committee' (*comissões paritarias de interpretação*) at the level on which the agreement is concluded. This must comprise equal numbers from the employers and trades unions but may also include outside experts. The possibility that a committee with this composition could succeed where the parties to the agreement have failed is seen as remote. Thus this is often considered a bureaucratic procedure, made even more complicated by the plurality of unions, which yields poor results. If the committee unanimously agrees to a decision, then it has the same force as a collective agreement. The Ministry of Labour may be requested to participate in the interpretation though it has no voting powers. This is a cheaper, but often less effective, remedy than resort to the courts, though delays can last between one and two years. Since the interpretation committee is an integral part of a legally binding collective agreement, industrial action is not normally conducted in pursuit of such issues. The labour courts can be asked to interpret clauses of a collective agreement at any time, and their decision is binding.

Conciliation, mediation, arbitration

These procedures deal with *conflicts of interest*. If no prior conciliation procedure has been agreed by parties to an agreement, the services of the Ministry of Labour may be called upon by joint agreement or even under some circumstances by just one party. The procedure must be triggered within fifteen days of the date of the receipt of the reference. The procedure is frequently used but generally produces no positive result. Conciliators are officials of the labour ministry and often closely identified with the party political interests represented in government. Since they have no legal powers to force the parties to reach agreement but merely encourage them to make mutual concessions, conciliation is not usually very effective.

An optional mediation procedure is also outlined in legislation, under which an outside mediator may be chosen by the parties, who must put forward a proposition within a twenty-day period. This method of resolving disputes is rarely employed.

Arbitration is hardly ever used, partly on grounds of expense. Statute law lays down that each side may choose one arbitrator, and the two arbitrators together select a third. The arbitration committee may be assisted by outside experts. Awards, which must be by majority, have the same force in law as collective agreements. Arbitration is sometimes compulsory for public undertakings.

The Ministry of Labour is reviewing the whole dispute resolution procedure with a view to extensive reform. This could involve compulsory arbitration in some circumstances.

Collective dismissal

One crucial area where a company has to inform, consult

and negotiate with the workers' committees is over collective dismissals. Since Portugal joined the EC only in 1986, there are some transitional provisions regarding the transposition of directives into national law, with full compliance by the end of 1992. However, in the employment field Portuguese law on collective issues tends to be more stringent than EC requirements and therefore no major changes are envisaged.

The dismissal legislation was amended in 1989, giving employers more flexibility to make changes in their work force, for economic reasons in particular (see decree law 64-A/89, chapter v, Section 1 and the second volume in the European Management Guides series, *Terms and Conditions of Employment*).

Collective dismissal is defined as the termination of employment contracts on structural, technical or economic grounds, affecting at least two (or at least five) employees in enterprises with up to 50 (or more than 50) employees over a period of three months. This could be a total or partial closure of the enterprise, or a simple reduction in the numbers employed.

Management must *inform* the workers' committee, or in its absence the trade union committee, in writing of its intention to declare redundancies. It must give reasons (economic, technical or financial), details of the groups and departments affected, the criteria for selection (laid down by law) and the actual number of workers concerned and their skill category. The Ministry of Labour must also be informed, with supporting data, and is charged to ensure the dismissal procedure is properly conducted and to conciliate between the two sides as appropriate. It has the ultimate power to refuse redundancies but the power is rarely used.

Within fifteen days of communicating its intention to dismiss, management and the workers' committee must discuss and *negotiate* over possibilities of reducing the impact of the planned redundancy. Specifically they must consider the scope for short-time working, a reduction in working hours, temporary lay-off, reconverting skills and early retirement.

If the redundancy goes ahead, the company must, within thirty days of the original notification, inform the workers of their dismissal, giving the reasons and the date on which it will take effect. This cannot be less than sixty days after the date on which individuals were informed. During the period of notice workers are entitled to up to two days off a week to seek work, provided the employer is informed. A dismissal will be declared null and void if the procedure is not fully carried out.

On dismissal, employees have a right to compensation equivalent to one month's pay per year (or part year) of service, with a minimum payment of three months' wages.

Appendix

Ministry of Labour and Social Security (Ministério do Emprego e da Segurança Social):
Praça de Londres 2
Lisboa
tel. + 351 1 80 44 60

Institute of Employment and Vocational Training (Instituto do Emprego e Formação Profissional):
11 Avenida José Malhoa
Lisboa
tel. + 351 1 726 25 36

Association of Portuguese Human Resource Managers (Associação Portuguesa dos Gestores e Técnicos dos Recursos Humanos):
avenida do Brasil 194, 7°
1700 Lisboa
tel. + 351 1 89 97 66
fax + 351 1 80 93 40

Office in Oporto:
Rua Formosa 49, 1°
4000 Oporto
tel. + 351 2 32 32 34
fax + 351 2 200 07 64

Confederation of Portuguese Industry (Confederação da Indústria Portuguesa, CIP, central employers' organization for industry)
Avenida 5 de Outubro 35, 1°
1000 Lisboa
tel. + 351 1 54 74 54

Confederation of Portuguese Commerce (Confederação do Comércio Portuguêsa, CCP, central employers' organization in trade and commerce):
Rua Saraiva de Carvalho, 1–2°
1000 Lisboa
tel. + 351 1 66 85 39

British–Portuguese Chamber of Commerce:
Rua da Estrela 8
1200 Lisbon
tel. + 351 1 66 15 86

Confederação Geral dos Trabalhadores Portugueses – Intersindical Nacional (CGTP-IN)
Rua Vitor Cordon, 1–3°
1200 Lisboa
tel. + 351 1 34 72 181/8

União Geral de Trabalhadores (UGT)
Rua Buenos Aires II
1200 Lisboa
tel. + 351 1 67 65 03/5

10

Spain

The framework of modern industrial relations in Spain began in 1977 when Spain ratified ILO conventions 87 and 98, on the rights of association of workers and employers and on trade union guarantees. Article 28 of the constitution in 1978 then enshrined the principle of trade union rights. The Workers' Statute of 1980 defined the structure and procedures of industrial relations, stating, for example, that collective agreements must at least contain the minimum conditions defined in the Workers' Statute. In 1985 the Trade Union Freedoms Law extended and refined these provisions. These latter two pieces of legislation have shaped the structure of employee participation in the workplace through the system of works councils, workers' delegates and trade union branches, which give statutory rights of participation to employees in all companies or workplaces of more than ten employees.

However, although these statutory measures, supplemented by court rulings, have gradually installed a democratic system of industrial relations, there are still small but significant vestiges of provisions dating from the Franco dictatorship, which may on occasions be applicable: these are the 'Labour Ordinances', a code of conduct for each sector, which have largely been superseded by collective agreements but which can still have some minimal effect in certain cases.

National structures of tripartite co-operation

There is no single formal body at national level to agree tripartite co-operation, although for some years the government has promised to establish such a body, the Consejo Económico y Social, which in its draft constitution, issued in 1990, envisages a consultative assembly of government, employers and trade unions to consider aspects of economic and social policy.

There were a series of 'social contracts' in the past decade, which aimed to set a framework for bargaining. However, even though the last of these, the *Acuerdo Económico y Social*, included the government as well as the social partners, such framework agreements appear unlikely to return in the near future. In mid-1991, the government was attempting to secure agreement on a form of pact aimed at boosting national economic performance (*Pacto de Competitividad*).

Workplace employee representation

Workers have a right to be collectively represented under statutory systems of employee representation: the precise arrangements depend on establishment size.

Staff representatives and works councils

In smaller companies of ten to forty-nine employees, the work force is represented by staff representatives (*delegados de personal*). In larger workplaces, with fifty or more employees, representation is through works councils (*comités de empresa*).

Staff representatives are elected on the basis of one delegate for between eleven and thirty employees, and three delegates where there are thirty-one to forty-nine employees. In smaller companies or workplaces of six to ten employees, one delegate may be elected if a majority of employees wish it.

Works councils are elected by employees according to the following scale:

Work force size	*Works council members*
50–100	5
101–250	9
251–500	13
501–750	17
751–1,000	21

Above 1,000 employees, there are two members per thousand (or less), up to a maximum of seventy-five.

When a company has two or more workplaces in a province or

in adjoining municipalities, each of which has fewer than fifty employees but which together have fifty, then a joint works council is formed. When one workplace in this situation has fifty employees, and the others have not, then the workplace with fifty employees forms its own council and the others form one between them. It is permissible by collective agreement to form a joint works council linking several workplaces, with a maximum of thirteen members, whose functions are defined by collective agreement.

Staff representatives and works council members are elected by direct secret ballot by all employees aged over 16 with at least one month's service. Candidates must be over 18, with at least six months' service. Candidates for these elections are sponsored by the 'most representative' trade unions (that is, the UGT and CC.OO, and ELA–STV in the Basque country – see also below), by trade unions with a minimum 10 per cent representation in the work force, or by a majority nomination of the employees. In the case of staff representatives, each employee may vote for as many candidates as there are places, and the winners are those with the highest total votes. In the case of works councils, two electoral colleges are formed – one by technical and administrative staff and the other by specialist and unskilled staff. Each employee votes for a slate of candidates, and slates failing to reach 5 per cent of the votes from each college are eliminated.

Workers' delegates and works council members serve for a term of four years. Elections took place in 1990, and the next elections will be held in 1994. The two main unions, Unión General de Trabajadores (UGT) and Comisiones Obreras (CC.OO) accounted for the overwhelming majority of elected representatives in the 1990 elections, with the UGT accounting for 42 per cent and the CC.OO for 35 per cent of all elected representatives.

Rights and duties of works councils. The principal statutory right of work-force representatives is to receive information and to express an opinion on matters submitted to them. Works councils are also required to supervise employer compliance with current labour, social security and employment legislation, and to oversee health and safety conditions at the workplace. The council is obliged to warn the employer of dangerous or unhealthy working conditions (in the absence of a health and safety committee), and may suspend work if necessary when working circumstances present a threat to health or life, and the employer has not responded to earlier requests for aciton. Works councils and managements may also conclude agreements on any area they wish.

The main information and consultation rights are:

- To receive quarterly information on developments in the economic sector the company belongs to, reports on production and sales plans, and likely employment trends in the company.
- To receive company financial reports, annual reports and the same information which shareholders receive.
- To express an opinion before the employer takes action on work-force restructuring, redundancies, short-time working, total or partial transfers of workplaces, the implementation of time-and-motion studies, bonus systems and job evaluation, grading, flexi-time arrangements and shift working.
- To be informed of the model employment contracts used in the company and documents relating to termination of contracts.
- To receive quarterly reports on absenteeism, occupational accidents and sickness.
- To be informed of all sanctions imposed for very serious offences.
- To receive a copy of all fixed-term written employment contracts issued by the employer, so as to monitor the use of temporary employment contracts.
- To be informed of the company's plans for providing training for young recruits on training contracts.
- To be informed of the arrangements reached with the National Employment Institute (INEM) for work experience contracts.
- To receive monthly reports of overtime worked.

The committee may convene workplace meetings out of working time at least every two months and when one third of members or one third of the workplace call for a meeting.

Rights of work-force representatives. Elected work-force representatives enjoy a number of rights and guarantees. They are protected against dismissal or sanctions during the first year of office, and for one further year, when the reason for dismissal or sanction is connected with operations as an elected representative. There is also a right of appeal in the event of sanctions for a very serious or serious offence, to be made in the presence of the works council or the other worker delegates. Where redundancies are taking place on economic or technological grounds, elected representatives have priority in respect of safeguarding their employment and also enjoy protection in the event of relocation for technical or organizational reasons.

Representatives are free to express views on matters relating to their role as workers' representative, and to print and disseminate material of economic or social relevance, provided it does not interfere with normal working.

Each member of a works council or staff representative is entitled to paid time off to carry out their duties, with the amount of time off determined by workplace size. The monthly scale is as follows:

Work force	*Hours' leave per month*
–100	15
101–250	20
251–500	30
501–750	35
750+	40

These hours may be pooled, to allow certain delegates or works council members to devote more time to representation.

Right of assembly. The Workers' Statute grants the right of assembly to a work force, irrespective of works council or trade union procedures. Workers have the right to call a meeting – for example, to repeal the mandate of a works council (after due notice, when called by at least one-third of the work force) or to take decisions which affect the work force as a whole. Such an assembly cannot prejudice the lawful working of the works council. The employer must be given forty-eight hours' notice of the meeting, and the meeting must be chaired by the works council. The employer must be informed of the agenda and of the names of any non-employees who will be attending. The employer is obliged to allow the meeting to take place in the workplace, provided the legal requirements have been met and that at least two months have elapsed since the last meeting. Any decisions taken by the meeting must be by secret ballot, including postal ballot, with a simple majority of the work force deciding.

Health and safety committees

Current health and safety legislation dates from 1971, and has been partly incorporated into the Workers' Statute. However, the government intends to overhaul this legislation. Under the 1971 legislation, all workplaces with more than 100 employees – or fewer when 'specially dangerous activities' are concerned – are required to establish a health and safety committee, consisting of a chairperson appointed by the employer, a qualified health and safety technician and a qualified medical specialist, a member of staff qualified in first aid, the head of company safety, a number of elected staff representatives (three in companies with under 500 employees, four in companies of 500–1,000 employees, five in companies of 1,000 or more employees) and a secretary appointed from among the white-collar staff.

In workplaces with fewer than 100 employees, health and safety is the responsibility of the works council or the staff representatives. In the construction, ceramic and glass industries a health and safety committee must be established in companies with more than fifty employees. The committee must meet at least monthly, and twice yearly must also meet the company technicians, medical staff and middle management. It provides a monthly report to the provincial office of the Ministry of Labour.

Legislation passed in 1988 (Law 8/1988 of 7 April), which details employers' and employees' responsibilities and liabilities in a wide range of employment areas, identifies failure to constitute a health and safety committee in accordance with the law as a serious offence, liable to fines ranging from Pta 50,000 to Pta 500,000 (£275–2,750) – with an upper limit of Pta 15 million (£82,000) for repeated offences. Equally, the employer is empowered to discipline employees who disregard health and safety regulations. Sanctions range from verbal warnings for lesser offences to suspension without pay for up to two months and disbarring an employee from promotion for up to two years.

Trade unions

Trade union structure

There are two major trade union confederations and a large number of small unions or professional associations. Despite the active part played by trade unions in the construction of Spanish democracy, and their influential role in the determination of pay and conditions, trade union density is among the lowest in Europe, amounting to about 15 per cent of the work force. Nevertheless, the major union confederations have an influence substantially greater than their level of affiliation would imply, and they have considerable statutory protection under the Workers' Statute and the Trade Union Freedoms Law, which grant a strong institutional role to them, especially as regards collective bargaining and workers' representation.

The two dominant unions are the Unión General de Trabajadores (UGT) and Comisiones Obreras (CC.OO). The UGT, founded in 1889, has been the trade union base of the Spanish Socialist Party for a century. In 1990 it claimed 960,000 members, broken down into fourteen constituent federations; in the 1990 works council elections it gained 112,149 places (44 per cent of the total). Although the UGT is the larger of the two major trade unions, its strength lies in small and medium companies and in the public sector. CC.OO was formed in the mid-1960s and operated underground for the first decade of its existence. Although in its early period it attracted a broad grouping of anti-Franco members, including progressive Catholics and liberals, its main influence has been the Spanish Communist Party. In the 1990 works council elections it gained 91,919 places (36 per cent). In contrast to the UGT, CC.OO is most strongly represented in large companies – in the 1990 elections it gained 36,690 elected delegates in companies of more than fifty employees, against the 35,680 gained by UGT – and is particularly strong in private firms in banking, insurance, engineering, chemicals, health, teaching and printing. Like the UGT, CC.OO is organized into fourteen constituent federations.

The third largest union is Unión Sindical Obrera (USO), formed clandestinely in the 1960s, with a largely Socialist/liberal Catholic tradition. Although gaining 7,220 elected delegates in 1990, USO failed to reach the status of 'most representative union' (see below). It claimed some 87,000 members in 1990, and its strengths lie in engineering, mining, private education and the civil service. The Confederación General de Trabajo (CGT, CNT until a court ruling in 1989) has roots in the anarchist tradition which was strong in Spain in the late nineteenth and early twentieth centuries. It was a powerful force in the 1930s, with over a million members. Now it has some 20,000 members. Its strengths are in Catalonia and Valencia, and it has had recent local successes, even coming to control the works councils of Ford Valencia and the Barcelona Metro.

There are two regionally important unions. Confederación Sindical Euzko Laguillen Alkartasuna–Solidaridad de Trabajadores Vascos (ELA–STV) is the largest of the unions in the Basque country, claiming to represent some 8 per cent of unionized workers in Spain. In the 1990 elections it gained 7,325 places in the Basque country – more than the UGT or CC.OO. Central Intersindical Gallega (CIG) represents workers in Galicia, and claimed some 25,000 members in the late 1980s. Its strengths lie in engineering, construction, teaching, health care, the civil service, the timber trades and banking.

Apart from these major national and regional unions, there are some 344 smaller federations or associations, comprising professional groups, enterprise unions, etc., which in total gained some 20,344 places in the 1990 elections.

Rights of association

Although unions were active and politically influential earlier in the century, they were banned by General Franco during the period 1939–75. In 1977 the *Ley de Asociación Sindical* permitted freedom of association for both trade unions and employers' associations. The 1978 constitution enshrined the right of association and of trade union membership for all citizens except members of the armed forces, and the Workers' Statute elaborated further on the sphere of action of associations. The 1985 Trade Union Freedoms Law delineated the constitution and rights of trade unions. The law grants the following freedoms of association:

- The right to form trade unions without prior authorization, and the right to suspend or dissolve trade unions by democratic process.
- The right of employees to join the trade union of their choice or withdraw from membership: no one may be compelled to join a trade union.
- The right of members to freely elect trade union representatives.
- The right to carry on trade union activities.

Union dues may be deducted by the employer through a check-off system if a union requests it and provided the individual employee consents.

Trade union representation

Trades unions are entitled to form workplace branches, and to recruit, hold meetings, distribute information and collect dues outside working time. The 1985 legislation contains the concept of 'most representative trades union', which gives substantially better rights to large unions. Under this principle, unions which achieve 10 per cent nationally of the votes cast in the elections for workers' delegates or works council members (or 15 per cent in the respective Autonomous Community elections, provided at least 1,500 delegates are elected – a condition which applies largely to Galicia and the Basque country) are entitled:

- To participate in national-level collective bargaining.
- To take an active part in setting conditions of employment in the public sector through the appropriate machinery.
- To participate in mediation proceedings to settle industrial disputes.

This provision applies nationally to Comisiones Obreras and the Unión General de Trabajadores, to ELA–STV in the Basque country and to CIG in Galicia.

Employees who are members of unions have the right to form workplace trade union branches which participate in collective bargaining, have a right to a company notice-board, and to an office in workplaces with more than 250 employees. Workplaces with more than 250 employees may also have trade union delegates elected according to the following scale:

Size of work force	Number of union delegates
250–750	1
751–2,000	2
2,001–5,000	3
5,001+	4

A single delegate may represent any trade union which did not achieve 10 per cent of the votes for the works council members.

Union delegates have the same guarantees as works council members, and may attend works council meetings, health and safety meetings, etc., as non-voting members. They also have the right to express their views to the management on issues affecting the work force, especially as regards dismissals and sanctions affecting their members. An elected official at provincial, autonomous community or state level is entitled to unpaid time off. Members of bargaining commissions are granted paid time off, as required to fulfil their duties.

Legal status of trade unions

Trade unions have a legal personality and are answerable for acts carried out by duly established organs acting within their competence, but not for the individual acts of union members unless they are acting on behalf of the union. In order to acquire legal personality, which also includes tax concessions, and the capacity to bargain collectively, unions must register with the authorities. This entails lodging a copy of their internal rules, which are open to public inspection.

Employers' organizations

There is one major employers' confederation, the Confederación Española de Organizaciones Empresariales (CEOE). It comprises employers in the public and private sectors, with member firms accounting for nearly 10 million employees out of total work force of some 14 million. A sister organization, the Confederación Española de Pequeñas y Medianas Empresas (CEPYME) looks after the interests of small and medium companies.

An employers' organization can obtain the legal capacity to bargain collectively if it represents 10 per cent of employers nationally, or 15 per cent in an autonomous community.

Bargaining

Collective bargaining

Collective bargaining occurs at three levels: national sectoral, provincial sectoral, and undertaking. There are notably few national sectoral agreements; they exist in chemicals, small engineering workshops, banking, paper and board, insurance, and some foodstuffs sectors such as canned foods. There are a considerable number of agreements at provincial level: in 1990 1,285 such agreements covered 5,957,000 employees – over a third of the work force. Undertaking-level agreements, some 3,000 of which were registered in 1990, covered 1,051,600 employees. Some 68 per cent of agreements operate for one year and most of the remainder for two years: the chemicals agreement is exceptional in operating for three years. All agreements have their pay and conditions reviewed annually. It is possible under statute to have agreements extended to similar undertakings in the vicinity; this rarely happens, however, and generally only in sectors where there are many small workplaces such as retailing or small workshops.

The Workers' Statute sets out the conditions which have to be met for employee organizations if they are to have the capacity to engage in collective bargaining. Both parties must recognize the other as bargaining agents. Under the 1985 Trade Union Freedoms Law, trade unions have a right to bargain collectively. At national level, collective bargaining takes place between employers' representatives of the respective federation and the 'most representative unions', as defined above – in most instances the UGT and CC.OO. Collective bargaining takes place in negotiating committees, regulated by the Workers' Statue. At undertaking level, these consist of up to twelve members from each side, with fifteen representatives from each side for higher-level agreements: representation is guaranteed to any union or employers' organization fulfilling the criteria required to obtain the capacity to bargain collectively. An agreement must be approved by 60 per cent of the members of each side to become effective.

Negotiation begins by one party informing the other in writing of its desire to enter into discussions, specifying its representative status, the agreement in question, and the matters for negotiation. Negotiation can be refused only on grounds specified in law or by collective agreement, or where the discussions have a purpose other than that of renewing an agreement which has expired. There is a legal obligation to bargain in good faith.

Unless formal notice to terminate the agreement is given by one side, agreements are deemed to remain in force after their expiry date – which is normally 31 December. In practice it is normal for the trade union negotiators to register their intention to renegotiate in the last three months of the agreement. Formal notice to renegotiate must be lodged with the local offices of the Ministry of Labour; then the whole bargaining process is rather dilatory. While agreements almost always date from 1 January, bargaining does not often begin until February, when the retail price index from the previous year is known and official forecasts can be established. Negotiations can be protracted, lasting two to three months, with agreements becoming legally binding when they are published in a government official journal, the *Boletín Oficial del Estado* or the respective provincial equivalents, generally in June or later. In those few industries in which national sectoral agreements exist, the contents of the agreement define the minimum conditions which must apply in the provincial or company-level agreements which follow. In other sectors, bargaining at provincial level (or the Autonomous Regional level in the Basque country or Catalonia) sets the minimum level of conditions, which company agreements then adopt. In general, most lower-level agreements do no more than accept the minimum conditions set by the national or provincial agreement.

When there is disagreement over the interpretation of the terms of a collective agreement, minor matters are usually dealt with by the agreement monitoring committee (*comisión de seguimiento*) established by the agreement itself, or the works council. Serious disputes are handled by the labour courts (*juzgado de lo social*), with appeals to the Central Labour Tribunal and sometimes the Constitutional Tribunal when fundamental issues, such as sex discrimination on pay, are at stake.

Collective disputes

Under decree law 17/1977 it is not permissible to initiate a collective dispute to modify an existing collective agreement. However, following a 1981 ruling by the Constitutional Tribunal either employers or employees may initiate a collective dispute to modify or determine employment conditions or to interpret a previously agreed or decreed provision. The dispute may be initiated by the employees' or employers' legal representatives or by unions and employers' associations directly concerned with the point at issue. Such disputes must be presented in writing, adducing all the reasons for the dispute, to the labour authorities, who will call the two sides together with three days' notice. If agreement is reached on settling the dispute by a majority of the representatives present, this agreement will have the same binding effect as a collective agreement. In the event of a failure to agree, arbitrators may be appointed if both sides wish: the arbitrators must issue their binding ruling within five days. If there is no agreement or arbitration process, the labour authorities may send the dispute to the labour courts for resolution.

Employees may not take strike action while collective dispute procedures are being followed.

Mediation and conciliation

Although Spain has nominally had official means for resolving disputes since 1977 (the Instituto de Mediación, Conciliación y Arbitraje, IMAC), collective mediation and conciliation procedures never developed as originally hoped. The outcome is that although many of the Autonomous Community governments now have IMAC offices, these serve almost exclusively to resolve individual disputes. Collective disputes will generally be argued and resolved at the level of the courts, where case law is gradually being built up.

The one major exception to this pattern is the Basque country, where the major trade unions and the Basque Employers' Confederation (CONFEBASK) have established voluntary machinery which includes a register of arbitrators.

Industrial action

Strikes

At present the right to strike is guaranteed by the 1978 constitution. Specific legislation on industrial action is still pending, and at the moment the most authoritative ruling on strike law is a prior statute, decree law 17/1977. Some guidance on the interpretation of the decree law and the subsequent constitution, which clash on some issues, has been provided by a 1981 ruling of the Constitutional Tribunal (*sentencia* 11/81).

The decision to strike must be reached by an express decision of the work force, though no percentage figure is stipulated. The decision may be that of the staff representatives, the workers' delegates, the works council or the workplace unions – in all cases it must be a majority decision – or by the work force in general. Provisions of the 1977 decree law which prescribed exact percentages were declared unconstitutional. Five days' notice of a proposed strike must be given both to the employer and to the labour authorities. In the case of strikes in the public sector the period of notice is extended to ten days.

The strike committee must state the aims of the strike, measures taken to avoid it, the strike date and the composition of the strike committee. The strike committee may consist of up to twelve members elected from employees directly involved in the dispute. Among its duties are those of co-ordinating essential services which ensure the safety of people and plant, adequate maintenance of plant and raw materials and preparations necessary for later start-up.

When strikes are declared in public services or other essential services, the government is empowered to order the provision of minimum services but not necessarily to order a return to work.

Occupations of the workplace are unlawful, as are a number of types of strike action, including rolling strikes, strikes which interrupt production in strategic sectors, go-slows and working to rule, or any other form of collective industrial action other than an all-out strike. Similarly, political strikes, and strikes which cause disproportionate disruption, are also unlawful. Secondary action is permitted, according to case law.

Striking employees may not be replaced by other workers, and can publicize the strike and collect funds, but are not allowed to intimidate non-strikers. Engaging in a strike suspends the contract of employment but does not provide grounds for terminating it.

Lock-outs

Lock-outs are permissible when employers need to protect their basic interests. Such need may arise during a lawful or unlawful strike when there is danger of violence against persons or property, a danger of an occupation of the workplace, or such irregular attendance and production that normal working is impeded. The employer must inform the labour authorities of a lock-out within twelve hours, and it may last only the minimum time necessary. Lock-outs have the same effect as strike action, and suspend but do not terminate contracts of employment. A lock-out may be terminated by order of the labour authorities.

Collective dismissal

Collective redundancy and lay-off procedures are regulated by a series of laws (the Workers' Statute, law 32/1984, royal decree 696/1980, royal decree 2731/1981 and royal decree 521/1990). All collective redundancies involving more than one employee, lay-offs and short-time working are tightly controlled by statute. An employer wishing to take such measures must apply for authority to do so and receive approval (a *regulación de empleo*) from the employment authorities.

Statute law allows the following grounds for granting such requests:

- *Economic grounds:* when a company can demonstrate real objective financial difficulties.
- *Technological grounds:* when a company can demonstrate that it has to introduce technical changes for reasons of competitiveness.
- *Force majeure:* when unforeseen circumstances disrupt the normal pattern of business activity.
- *Termination* of the employer's legal operations.

An employer must address the request to the provincial head office of the Ministry of Labour, in the case of companies with fewer than 500 employees when the proposal affects no more than 200 employees. Otherwise the company must apply to the office of the Director General of Labour (or the appropriate department of the Autonomous Provincial government, when Labour Ministry affairs have been transferred to this office). In the case of permission sought for economic or technological reasons, the employer must give thirty days' notice to the workers' representatives for redundancies, or fifteen days' notice of lay-offs or short-time working, during which time there must be discussion between both sides. The employer must at the same time notify the employment authorities and forward to them a copy of the request for the *regulación de empleo*, together with all relevant financial and other documentation to support the request. If employer and employees do not reach agreement within the thirty days, and the employer proceeds with the request to the employment authorities, it must be accompanied by:

- A request submitted on the official form.
- Minutes of the discussions with the workers' representatives.
- A memo explaining the economic or technological reasons for the request.
- Financial documentation (balance sheets, accounts, tax returns).
- A report from the works council.
- An auditor's report (in companies with more than fifty employees).
- A report from the National Employment Institute (INEM) on the applicability of unemployment benefit to the employees affected.

In the case of *force majeure*, the request must be supported by any relevant documentation.

The employment authorities will request a report from the labour inspectorate and any other appropriate public bodies.

If agreement is reached between the employer and the workers' representatives, the employment authorities will rule within fifteen days in the case of redundancy and eight days in the case of lay-offs or short-time working. In cases of *force majeure* they will rule within five days. Appeals are allowed. If redundancies or lay-offs are authorized, compensation will be paid at a rate of twenty days' pay per year of service, to a maximum of twelve months' pay. In companies with fewer than twenty-five employees the government Wage Guarantee Fund will cover 40 per cent of compensation due. In the case of lay-offs the employment contracts are suspended and the employer is obliged to continue to pay social security contributions (except in cases of *force majeure*). In cases of short-time working the employment contract is suspended *pro rata* and the employer is liable for social security contributions *pro rata*.

Transfer of undertakings

Under the Workers' Statute, transfer of ownership of a company, workplace or unit of production does not terminate an employment relationship. The new owner inherits the employment rights and obligations of the old owner. The existing owner is obliged to notify the workers' representatives of the change of ownership, and both transferor and transferee are jointly liable for a further three years for any undischarged obligations arising out of the employment relationship prior to the transfer.

Appendix

Ministry of Labour and
Social Security.
(Ministerio de Trabajo y
Seguridad Social):
Agustín de Bethencourt 4
28003 Madrid
tel. + 34 1 253 6000/253 7600
fax + 34 1 233 2996

INEM (Instituto Nacional
de   Empleo,   the   National
Employment Institute):
Calle Condesa de Venadito 9
28027 Madrid
tel. + 34 1 585 9888
fax + 34 1 268 3981/268 3982

Asociación Española de
Directores de Personal (AEDIPE),
(the Spanish Association of
Personnel Directors):
Moreto 10
28010 Madrid
tel. + 34 1 468 2217

Confederación Española de
Organizaciones Empresariales
(CEOE) (the Spanish employers'
organization):
Diego de León 50
28006 Madrid
tel. + 34 1 563 9641
fax + 34 1 262 8023

Unión General de Trabajadores
(UGT)
Hortaleza 88
Madrid
tel. + 34 1 308 3333

Comisiones Obreras (CC.OO)
Fernández de la Hoz 6
28010 Madrid
tel. + 34 1 419 5454

Selected further reading

Comparative studies

CHRISTEL LANE, *Management and Labour in Europe* (Edward Elgar, Aldershot, 1989) compares industrial relations, vocational training, managerial style and control, job design and work organization in Britain, France and Germany.

MICHAEL GOLD/MARK HALL, *Information and Consultation in European Multinational Companies: An evaluation of practice* (Dublin, 1991). Available from: European Foundation for the Improvement of Living and Working Conditions, Loughlinstown House, Co. Dublin, (tel. + 353 1 2826888).

International law and human rights at the workplace

ANGELA BYRE, *Human Rights at the Workplace* (PSI, London, 1988) draws together international law, including EC provisions, on a wide range of employment issues such as collective labour relations and trade union rights.

Recent literature on individual countries

On France:

CLAUDE PIGANIOL, 'Industrial relations and enterprise restructuring in France' in *International Labour Review*, Vol. 128, No. 5 (1989), 621–38.

YVES DELAMOTTE, 'Workers participation and personnel policies in France', in *International Labour Review*, Vol. 127, No. 2 (1988), 221–41.

JEFF BRIDGFORD, 'French trades unions: crisis in the 1980s', in *Industrial Relations Journal*, Vol. 21, No. 2 (Summer 1990), 126–35.

On the Irish Republic:

BRIAN WILKINSON, 'The Irish Industrial Relations Act 1990 – Corporatism and Conflict Control', in *Industrial Law Journal*, March 1991.

On Italy:

GUIDO BAGLIONI, 'An Italian mosaic: collective bargaining patterns in the 1980s', in *International Labour Review*, Vol 130, No. 1 (1991), 81–93.